PARTY
LINES

PARTY LINES

LINES

Competition,
Partisanship, and
Congressional
Redistricting

Thomas E. Mann and Bruce E. Cain
Editors

BROOKINGS INSTITUTION PRESS
Washington, D.C.

Copyright © 2005
THE BROOKINGS INSTITUTION
1775 Massachusetts Avenue, N.W., Washington, D.C. 20036
www.brookings.edu

Library of Congress Cataloging-in-Publication data

Party lines : competition, partisanship, and congressional redistricting / Thomas E.
Mann and Bruce E. Cain, editors.
   p. cm.
   Summary: "Details the legal and political history of redistricting since the
inception of the 'one person, one vote' rule, documenting its impact on competition,
polarization, and partisan fairness, and analyzes options for reform"—Provided by
publisher.
   Includes bibliographical references and index.
   ISBN-13: 978-0-8157-5468-8 (cloth : alk. paper)
   ISBN-10: 0-8157-5468-X (cloth : alk. paper)
   ISBN-13: 978-0-8157-5467-1 (pbk. : alk. paper)
   ISBN-10: 0-8157-5467-1 (pbk. : alk. paper)
   1. United States. Congress. House—Election districts.   2. Election districts—
United States.   3. Apportionment (Election law)—United States—History—20th
century.   I. Mann, Thomas E.   II. Cain, Bruce E.

   JK1341.P37 2005
   328.73'07345—dc22   2005024216

9 8 7 6 5 4 3 2 1

The paper used in this publication meets minimum requirements of the
American National Standard for Information Sciences—Permanence of Paper for
Printed Library Materials: ANSI Z39.48-1992.

Typeset in Adobe Garamond

Composition by R. Lynn Rivenbark
Macon, Georgia

Printed by R. R. Donnelley
Harrisonburg, Virginia

Contents

Foreword

At the core of a healthy democracy—just as at the core of what we do at Brookings—is the free and fair contest of ideas. For that principle to work in the political life of our nation, elections have to be genuinely contested. For the vast majority of seats in the U.S. Congress, that just isn't happening. Only about 10 percent of the 435 districts feature a serious campaign between two qualified and well-financed candidates in which the outcome is uncertain. The last two elections set records for the smallest number of House incumbents defeated by challengers in a general election.

This extraordinarily high level of incumbent safety and precipitous decline in competitiveness has been accompanied by growing ideological polarization and bitter struggle between the parties to achieve or maintain majority control of the House. These developments have poisoned public life in Washington and complicated the challenges of governance.

Many analysts believe that redistricting—the process by which legislative district boundaries are redrawn after each decennial census—lies at the root of the problem. This volume, which grew out of a conference at Brookings in 2004, systematically assesses that claim. Its editors, Tom Mann, W. Averell

Harriman Chair and senior fellow at Brookings, and Bruce Cain, director of the Institute of Governmental Studies at the University of California–Berkeley, conclude that gerrymandering is only one of the forces responsible for the ills associated with contemporary congressional elections and that redistricting reform is no guarantee of finding a more competitive and less polarized national politics. It is not, however, an unreasonable place to start the search. Tom and Bruce and their colleagues therefore suggest how that effort might best unfold.

This volume is part of a larger effort at Brookings to analyze the causes and consequences of gerrymandering and to lead a national debate on how redistricting processes can be improved. We are grateful to the Carnegie Corporation, the Joyce Foundation, and the Cabot Family Charitable Trust for their support of this ambitious project.

STROBE TALBOTT
President

Washington, D.C.
September 2005

PARTY
LINES

Introduction

The essence of any democratic regime is the competitive election of officeholders. It is only by making candidates compete for their seats that politicians can be held accountable by the public. In the American system, the framers of the Constitution envisioned that one governing body—the House of Representatives—would be especially responsive to the preferences and needs of the citizenry. In George Mason's words, the House "was to be the grand depository of the democratic principles of the government." Yet ironically, it is "the People's House" that has gradually become the representative institution least subject to electoral competition. The roots of this curious change are complex, but one critical element is the peculiar means by which congressional district boundaries are drawn in the United States. The redistricting process—its evolution, abuse, and impact on American democracy—is the subject of this book.

Redistricting is for the most part a subject of cyclical interest. Interest in the line-drawing process grows toward the end of every decade in anticipation of a new census and the reapportionment of congressional seats. In the run-up to a new round of redistricting, national parties battle to improve their electoral control of states where opportunities are ripe for seat gains or losses, while states organize themselves for the upcoming task, legislators jockey for positions on key redistricting committees, technical consultants ready their wares for sale, journalists bone up on the issue, and reformers hold numerous conferences in the hope of improving what seems to them to be an excessively political procedure.

But even in the quiet interval between censuses, there are occasional flare-ups. Between 1982 and 1993 and into the 1990s, in the heyday of aggressive enforcement of the Voting Rights Act (VRA), the Justice Department and minority advocacy groups challenged many existing electoral arrangements, including district lines, at all levels. Contested jurisdictions often capitulated in the face of expensive litigation, redrawing their lines mid-cycle. In other instances, some states could not resolve their districting problems politically and ended up in drawn-out legal cases involving both state and federal issues. Occasionally, those legal matters were not finally resolved until several years after the census.

The 2000 round of redistricting deviated a bit from the usual pattern. There was far less VRA controversy than many had predicted. Political jurisdictions were somehow able to steer a course between the "Don't do too little" commandment of *Thornburg* v. *Gingles* (1986),[1] which set the criteria under which majority-minority districts were to be drawn, and the "Don't do too much" commandment of *Shaw* v. *Reno* (1993) and its progeny,[2] which prohibited using race as the predominant factor in line drawing. A few large states that had experienced acrimonious partisan redistricting in the past, such as California, surprised many observers by achieving bipartisan agreement when they could have done otherwise. (Of course, there remained some states, such as Pennsylvania, Michigan, and Georgia, that followed the familiar pattern of producing partisan plans.) Since screams of outrage most often come from minority party elected officials and party activists, the prevalence of more bipartisan plans, especially in the larger states, had the effect of muting the controversy that usually followed previous rounds of line drawing. Bipartisan plans brought about more bipartisan satisfaction and fewer audible complaints from the usual suspects.

But the calm did not last for long. With a narrowly divided Congress and an increasingly partisan agenda, the Republicans, led by House Majority Leader Tom DeLay, opted to take advantage of a mid-decade opportunity to draw lines in Texas more to their liking. Despite a valiant attempt to run and hide, Texas Democrats could only stall the inevitable. Representative DeLay had his way, and the Republican legislature in Texas was able to transform a more neutral court plan into a more partisan Republican one that resulted in six more Republican seats. (One Democratic incumbent switched parties, another resigned, and four were defeated in the general election.) Suddenly the norm of redistricting tranquility between decades was under siege: if there was political advantage to be had, why wait?

At the same time, the strikingly uncompetitive 2002 and 2004 elections and the gradual erosion of September 11 unity caused observers to take a second look at the consequences of bipartisan plans. If bipartisan plans made incumbents in both parties safer, was it possible that they were making state legislatures and Congress more ideological at the same time? Ironically, plans that aim at bipartisan accord might actually produce more partisan discord if safe seats contribute to more ideological extremism, and, vice versa, partisan plans might make the districts of at least the majority party a little less safe and hence more moderate on the margin. Observers began to ask whether the prevalence of bipartisan redistricting played a part in the polarization of the federal and state legislatures.

One role of this volume is to take stock of what is known about the polarization question and to look more broadly at the issue of redistricting reform. If the process is defective, then the time to fix it is mid-decade—before political actors begin to view the whole issue in light of how it affects particular districts and their political careers.

Besides partisan acrimony and the mid-decade redistricting issue, two other features of the American legislative approach to redistricting have long bothered reformers, especially in light of data and software innovations. First, except for the handful of states with commission systems or those where the courts draw district lines because of a breakdown in the political system, state legislators vote on their own lines and U.S. House incumbents and the national parties work closely with them to draw congressional lines. Some critics believe that this practice creates a conflict of interest, arguing that drawing the boundaries of the districts in which they run gives legislators a personal "benefit" analogous to the benefit that they might gain by voting on legislation that might affect businesses or property that they own. Skeptics of that view note that an expanded definition of conflict of interest such as this opens the door to saying that any legislative vote that earns popular votes potentially creates a conflict of interest. Whatever position one takes, legislature-drawn lines indisputably give incumbents some ability, constrained by law and geography, to define their electoral battleground, and that can be unfair to challengers or minority parties.

Second, as with much legislation, significant parts of legislative plans are designed in secret, beyond public view, and give short shrift to public submissions. In contrast, state redistricting commissions, as in Arizona, and city redistricting commissions, as in San Diego or San Francisco, allow much more transparency. With advances in computer technology, more members of the public have access to redistricting data and software and appropriately demand to have their ideas for drawing districts heard. Both of these criticisms of the usual legislative procedures raise the question of whether there is a better way to draw lines.

This volume seeks to answer that question and to review the evolution—legal, technical, and political—of redistricting over the last several decades. The first chapter, by Bruce E. Cain, Karin Mac Donald, and Michael McDonald, looks at the shifting redistricting debate over time, arguing that the current period marks the resolution of most federal issues and the emergence of state and local considerations such as the requirement to create competitive seats or to take account of communities of interest. Chapter 1 also considers whether redistricting has lessened congressional competition and finds some evidence that it has.

If competition has lessened because of redistricting, what are the implications for American democracy? One effect is ideological polarization, as discussed, but there may be others as well. In chapter 2, L. Sandy Maisel, Cherie D. Maestas, and Walter J. Stone explore the idea that legislative redistricting may also decrease the number of strong candidates willing to run for office, thereby depriving voters of a full range of choices. Drawing from their Candidate Emergence Study, the authors find evidence of a connection between boundary changes, potential candidates' expectations of winning, and their likelihood of running. Maisel, Maestas, and Stone express concern that any process that favors incumbents and party interests will diminish competition and the quality of candidates.

Redistricting is ultimately a technical task: lines are drawn on the basis of census data, geographical units, and political returns. In large states, that fact can lead to huge data sets and complex technical considerations. In the 1970s and 1980s, much of the work was done by hand, which limited the ability of line drawers to negotiate and share information. In chapter 3, Micah Altman, Karin Mac Donald, and Michael McDonald trace the evolution of the software and data used in redistricting and suggest that it has increased the speed and accuracy of the process. They find that the implications of that increase are important but do not necessarily substantiate pundits' claims or the fears expressed by the courts.

Legal thinking on redistricting has changed almost as dramatically as the software. At the beginning of the 2000 round of redistricting, there was considerable speculation about how court rulings in the late 1990s would affect the implementation of the Voting Rights Act. In chapter 4, Nathaniel Persily examines that issue and also the latest attempt to interest the Supreme Court in political gerrymandering, *Vieth* v. *Jublierer*.[3] Reviewing the legal developments that led to the current state of redistricting law, Persily discusses how persistent tensions—between rules and standards, activism and restraint, individual and group rights—have created a confusing and inconsistent legal picture. This "massive superstructure of constraints" on district line drawing at all levels still allows a lot of room for political bargaining.

Thomas E. Mann concludes the volume with chapter 5, wherein he looks at the options for reform. While he reviews a wide range of potential constitutional, statutory, and judicial levers for change at the federal and state levels, he focuses especially on the experiences of redistricting commissions. Mann argues that the time might be ripe for taking redistricting out of the hands of state legislatures and giving it to independent commissions such as the one in Arizona. It is desirable and possible, he concludes, to embrace methods of redistricting that lie somewhere between an entirely neutral, apolitical process, one notably short on practical wisdom, and the ordinary political process, whose results are notably short on public interest.

Notes

1. *Thornburg* v. *Gingles*, 478 U.S. 30 (1986).
2. *Shaw* v. *Reno*, 509 U.S. 630 (1993).
3. *Vieth* v. *Jublierer*, 124 S. Ct. 1769 (2004).

1

From Equality to Fairness: The Path of Political Reform since *Baker* v. *Carr*

BRUCE E. CAIN, KARIN MAC DONALD, AND MICHAEL MCDONALD

The journey from *Baker* v. *Carr* in 1962 to the present has resembled a lengthy, hesitant walk through a maze more than the quick, straightforward trip to reform that some had hoped it might be. It seems on the surface that redistricting should be a simple, arithmetical task: making district populations as equal as possible so that everyone's vote counts the same. But the path to representational equality led to unforeseen destinations and several dead ends. Invoking the Constitution's equal protection clause in order to knock down malapportionment, the Warren Court unleashed a powerful principle on the murky, political enterprise of district boundary drawing. The principle of the right to an equally weighted vote has gradually morphed into other less well-defined or more controversial rights, such as to fair and effective representation, proportionate representation, nonretrogression, nonexclusion, nondilution, and now, perhaps, competitive seats.

The Supreme Court explicitly rejected some of these claims (for example, the right to proportionate shares for political parties and protected minorities). Others survived both constitutional scrutiny and the rough and tumble of real world application (for example, the section 5 protection against retrogression in the Voting Rights Act). Some redistricting claims were never defined clearly enough to be implemented (for example, the right to fair and effective representation). Now, new ones, such as the demand for competitive elections, are on the horizon.

Other aspects of redistricting have changed since 1962 as well. In 2001 the political conditions for line drawing differed in important ways from those of earlier decades. More large states had a divided government in 2001, altering the political deals struck in their state capitals so that redistricting plans became more bipartisan than before. In addition, more groups and individuals can now draw and analyze maps by computer and a greater number of states allow the public to participate by submitting plans for consideration.

This chapter offers an interpretation of redistricting reform in the United States since *Baker* v. *Carr*, emphasizing the interrelated changes among the legal, technological, and political factors involved. First, we delineate some phases of the redistricting evolution and attempt to explain why some reforms failed while others succeeded. Then we analyze the current issue of competitive seats in the context of that evolution. Last, we comment on some of the problems associated with achieving more competitiveness through redistricting.

The Long, Twisting Path toward Redistricting Reform

Much has happened and changed since the decision in *Baker* v. *Carr*. It is not our intent to provide a comprehensive summary of all those events, but we do think that it is valuable to characterize the changes in broad terms and to try to understand the lessons that they have to offer. That is particularly important as what seems to be a third wave of redistricting reform approaches, one focused on state criteria and the problem of rising partisanship in the United States. Over the years some redistricting reforms have succeeded; some have not. It is useful to speculate on why that is so. We describe three eras of redistricting reform: the apportionment period (1962–81), the vote dilution period (1982–93), and the nonfederal criteria period (1994 to the present), noting the legal, political, and technical state of affairs in each era and the lessons that can be gleaned from them.

The Apportionment Era (1962–81)

Contemporary redistricting reform began with the Supreme Court's decision in *Baker* v. *Carr*, which subjected redistricting and apportionment to legal scrutiny under Article 1, section 2, and the equal protection clause of the Constitution.[1] *Baker* v. *Carr* was a judicial reaction to a seemingly non–self-correcting political problem, which was that it was sometimes to the political advantage of certain groups in power to postpone redistricting and allow districts to become mal-apportioned. Overturning the precedent in *Colegrove* v. *Green* is in retrospect as revolutionary as it appeared to be at the time.[2] It opened up the door to a whole wave of judicial involvement in political matters, the most dramatic example being the Supreme Court's influence on the outcome of the 2000 presidential election.

It is safe to say that the *Baker* majority could not have foreseen how powerful the equal protection clause would become in American political reform. Judging from the evidence of notes and memoranda at the time, Chief Justice Earl Warren became convinced that it was simply unfair for the votes of some to count less than those of others.[3] He was less focused on the likely outcomes and political consequences of judicial intervention than on the principle of fairness.

The "one person, one vote" criterion as applied to line drawing emerged out of subsequent cases: *Wesberry* v. *Sanders* (1964) for congressional districts, *Reynolds* v. *Sims* (1964) for state legislative seats, and *Avery* v. *Midland County* (1968) for general purpose local governments.[4] Those decisions had two important effects on the American system of representation. First, they made population equality the highest redistricting priority. That meant that no matter how strongly a community or state felt about other legitimate goals, such as preserving city and county boundaries or respecting communities of interest, those criteria could not take priority over population equality. To put it another way, all other goals had to be implemented within the constraint of equal population of districts.

The equal population criterion inevitably wreaked havoc on geographic representation since in many instances homogeneous communities of interest had to be split or combined in order to achieve population equality among districts. The Court has allowed for greater flexibility in state redistricting when a good justification can be presented—for example, in *Abate* v. *Mundt* (1971); *Mahan* v. *Howell* (1973); *Brown* v. *Thomson* (1983); *Voinovich* v. *Quilter* (1993).[5] But it also has been suspicious when populations deviate more than plus or minus 5 percent without acceptable reasons, as it was in *Swann* v. *Adams* (1967). The pressure in congressional redistricting, on the other hand, has been in the direction of zero deviation, with little flexibility: *Kirkpatrick* v. *Preisler* (1969) and *White* v. *Weiser* (1973).[6]

As the dates of those cases indicate, the population deviation issue was settled pretty quickly and has not been modified much in the intervening decades. The concept was clear (even if, as some think, misguided), and it could be simply measured. The need for clarity and the tendency of political actors to abuse what is unclear drove the Court to a fairly bright and inflexible test: population deviations among districts had to fall within a given range unless local jurisdictions had a compelling and unusual reason to make district lines conform to local boundaries.

The second effect of the apportionment revolution was to wipe out geographically based upper-house representation for all but the U.S. Senate. Given that Chief Justice Warren had previously defended non–population-based districts as a reform device for controlling "bossism" in California, the Court's decision (written by Chief Justice Warren) in *Reynolds* and its companion cases was quite a shocking reversal. It had several effects on redistricting. At a minimum, it created more work, because now state upper-house as well as lower-house boundaries had to be redrawn after the decennial census to create equally populated districts. It also introduced many practical problems that states previously had not worried about much: When do representatives running in staggered terms (as many upper houses required) officially represent newly drawn areas within their districts? Does the assignment of a new district number change the date when an incumbent must run for reelection? Should lower-house seats be nested within the boundaries of upper-house lines?

A third effect of the apportionment revolution was the restructuring of some state constitutions and state statutes to ensure that districts would be redistricted in a timely fashion to comply with equal population requirements. Malapportionment was a concern as early as 1851, when Ohio adopted the first redistricting commission in the United States in order to conduct state legislative redistricting to handle population imbalances caused by westward migration into the state. The same motivation pertained for the thirteen states that adopted some form of commission system for their congressional or state legislative districts between 1963 and 1977. Other states wrote provisions for timely redistricting and requirements for equal population into their constitutions or state codes.

What were the important lessons of the apportionment era? First and foremost, the courts would now be looking over the shoulders of line drawers, and any redistricting plan, even one involving state legislative and local government districts, could be thrown out for violating the Constitution. Two, equal protection was a powerful principle that rapidly extended from federal to local districts and from district populations to the configuration of bicameral legislatures. It could mow down conventional and widely accepted practices if they did not conform to the norm of population equality. Three, equal population did not mean that unfairness was eliminated. The 1981 congressional redistricting, for example, featured the Phillip Burton California partisan redistricting plan, which added five seats to the Democratic caucus while conforming to the equal population requirement very strictly. By the end of the 1970s and the early 1980s, reformers concluded that "fair and effective" representation, however defined, required more than equally populated districts and equally weighted votes. But what? The litigation prompted by the 1981 redistricting took up that question in the vote dilution reform era.

Politically, there was a great deal of speculation that the apportionment revolution would help urban areas more than rural ones and Democrats more than Republicans. Since Republicans dominated in rural areas and Democrats in urban ones, logically the one-person, one-vote rule would bolster the Democratic Party's share of representation. The reapportionment revolution erased a pro-Republican bias among congressional districts.[7] However, Republican growth in the suburbs tempered partisan gains by the Democrats.[8] But that is not to say that there were no important shifts. Rural areas had less control over policymaking, and there were measurable changes in terms of policy and program spending.[9]

It was also politically significant that the Court rejected challenges to the population basis of redistricting. Given that nonvoters and noncitizens are more prevalent in poor and minority areas, there would have been a significant shift in representation had the Court allowed jurisdictions to redistrict on the basis of registered voters or even age-eligible citizens. But the Court rejected those claims and has accepted non-census data as a substitute only under specific conditions (see *Burns v. Richardson*, 1966).[10] On the other hand, the courts have not compelled jurisdictions to use data that purport to fix undercount problems, allowing Republican-controlled administrations in 1991 and 2001 to temporarily block the distribution of sampled data that would have adjusted for the undercount. Since the corrected data were widely perceived to favor the Democratic areas, Republicans were not interested in handing their opposition a significant electoral bonus. Given the problems associated with sampling and correcting the data, the courts upheld the federal government's decisions in 1991 and 2001 to require the use of uncorrected census data in line drawing.

Toward the end of this era and by the 1981 round of redistricting, the political system had pretty much adapted to the new rules. Computers were beginning to appear on the scene, and several states had the capacity to draw lines by precincts or census blocks and tracts with faster, more accurate technology. The California and New Jersey congressional plans illustrated how the political game could be played within the new demographic rules. The New Jersey lines left just enough population deviation (0.6984 percent) for the Court to intervene (*Karcher* v. *Daggett*, 1983) while the California plan (which was much more partisan) withstood challenges because it had virtually no population deviations.[11]

Even though new technology was starting to make its way into redistricting during this period, the process was still primarily closed. Public input was largely confined to the pre-decision phase and to post-plan comment; very few outside groups had the capacity to analyze legislatures' proposals, let alone submit a plan of their own. That meant little transparency and minimal public participation. Secrecy allowed for more backroom negotiation and compromise, with both good and bad consequences. Changing district lines in the era before computers was an onerous task, and had the state legislatures wanted greater public input (which on the whole they did not), it would have been difficult technically to involve the public and incorporate its changes in a timely manner.

The second important lesson of the apportionment era was that incumbency played a significant role in plan development. States had not yet passed term limits, and several large state legislatures had become highly professionalized. Professionalization meant larger salaries, pension systems, more staff support, and politics as a full-time career. Legislators at all levels learned how to use their franking privilege and district staff to build a personal vote, adding to the natural advantages of money and incumbency that come with officeholding. Reelection rates went up; turnover went down. Watergate drove down Republican support in many states, but when the GOP's fortunes turned up again toward the end of the Carter administration, it did not always translate into dramatic gains in state legislative and congressional district shares. Understandably, that fanned Republican frustration in the 1980s and led lawyers for the Republican National Convention (RNC) to become staunch advocates for redistricting reform.

An important point to note here, which we refer to later, is that incumbency considerations did not always mesh with partisan considerations.

Sometimes incumbents wanted areas because they were familiar or because they offered other advantages (for example, ease of fundraising). That made the task of drawing partisan-efficient lines more difficult. It was more natural to trade across party lines, with Democrats trading away their Republican areas for more Democratic ones, and vice versa.

Finally, bipartisan accommodation in the apportionment period did not have the bad image that it currently has. In *Gaffney* v. *Cummings* (1973), the Court held that maintaining a fair balance of Democrats and Republicans might be a legitimate state purpose, that there could be legitimate reasons for preserving existing district arrangements to the greatest extent possible, and that plans could try to allow incumbents fair opportunities for reelection.[12] Less consideration went into the more contemporary problem—that bipartisan plans tend to make each party's seats safer and more homogeneous. The more serious perceived unfairness at the time was that of the controlling party using redistricting to gain electoral advantage over the other.

The Vote Dilution Era (1982–93)

By the early 1980s, the redistricting reform frontier had moved past the simple goal of attaining equal populations. If anyone seriously thought that the one-person, one-vote constraint could cabin political mischief, the 1981 redistrictings dispelled that illusion. Small to nonexistent population deviations ruled out some options but left plenty of ways that one group or party could gain advantage over another. The right to an equally weighted vote, once achieved, did little to remedy the most common kinds of political unfairness inherent in legislative redistricting. The Court's attempt in 1983 to use population deviations as a pretext for striking down partisanship was restricted to Congress and easily evaded, as discussed earlier. Reformers asked whether additional constraints might be necessary. Could equal protection prevent one party from claiming more than its fair share of seats?

Those who sought to achieve greater representation for racial minorities were running into the limitations of Fourteenth Amendment litigation. Required by the Court to show that a particular redistricting was intended to be discriminatory (*Mobile* v. *Bolden*, 1980) and that it met the totality-of-circumstances test (*White* v. *Regester*, 1973), civil rights advocates felt stymied in their pursuit of fuller political representation for historically underrepresented groups.[13] If the apportionment era began with a judicial bolt of lightening (*Baker* v. *Carr*), the vote dilution era began with dramatic legislative action (the 1982 revision of the Voting Rights Act) and the prolonged partisan bickering that followed the 1981 round of redistricting.

The underlying legal right was relatively clear in the apportionment cases and a more or less bright-line test could be found, but neither the right nor the measure was obvious with respect to either racial or partisan vote dilution. What is an undiluted vote? The simplest answer, used in many other democracies in the world, would say that an undiluted vote yields a proportionate share for a party or racial group: if a group receives X percent of the vote, it should get X percent of the seats as well.[14] But there were problems with this potential bright-line test. First, it is hard to hold a district-based, single-member, simple plurality (SMSP) system to a proportional standard. A SMSP system by its nature tends to exaggerate the seat share of the larger party and to severely punish dispersed minority groups or parties. Even within proportional representation systems, strict proportionality is a myth; it is never achieved because of electoral thresholds and the inherent lumpiness of seat allocations.[15] Moreover, a standard based on vote shares is not obviously the right one for a redistricting based on population. Areas that are equally populated might not have equal numbers of age-eligible citizens if they also have disproportionate shares of minors or noncitizens in them. And most important, the Court itself refused to require proportionality in either partisan or racial representation.

If not proportionality, then what? The options were nonexclusion, rough proportionality, and symmetry or bias estimations. The first option, nonexclusion, was the default standard for both partisan and racial gerrymandering. In the partisan case, *Davis* v. *Bandemer* (1986), the Court declared that partisan gerrymandering could be justiciable, but it set the bar so high that it effectively killed all attempts to use the equal protection clause that way.[16] The major parties had to show "evidence of continued frustration of the will of the majority of the voters or effective denial to a minority of voters of a fair chance to influence the political process." Since it was a rare occurrence for a majority to be drawn into a minority (since they can "referend" bad plans in direct democracy states or elect a governor who will veto an unfavorable redistricting bill), the more likely prospect was a systematic lock-out or exclusion of the minority party. But that, too, has been rare in the United States since the breakup of the one-party South; the "out" party usually holds the governor's office or one branch of the legislature at some point in each decade.[17] Exclusion of the Democratic and Republican parties in this country is more a theoretical possibility than a recurrent reality.

With respect to racial vote dilution, the earliest victories in the wake of the amended Voting Rights Act (VRA) and *Thornburg* v. *Gingles* began with cases in which protected groups were shut out of representation entirely, but by the late 1980s, the second option, the rough proportionality standard, was informally adopted.[18] Applying the *Gingles* criteria, if an area contained a sufficiently large concentration of a protected group (a minimum of 50 percent), if there was evidence that its members voted as a coherent bloc, and if voting patterns were racially polarized, a jurisdiction could be obliged to draw additional majority-minority districts even when members of the protected group held office at the time of the redistricting. An informal expectation developed, based on Justice Department reviews and lower-court decisions, that if a majority-minority district could be drawn, it should be. That expectation weighed heavily in mapdrawing, since jurisdictions typically wanted to avoid the expense and turmoil of having their plans challenged and overturned by a court or the Justice Department. While the Court eschewed actual proportionality, the process itself developed the informal norm of rough proportionality. Rough proportionality meant that one drew as many majority-minority seats as one could within the *Gingles* parameters. That practice was eventually limited in important ways by the *Shaw* line of cases, marking the end of the vote dilution era.

The third option that the Court might have chosen, the symmetry standard, would have been more conceptually compatible with an SMSP system. However, it is not a simple bright-line test. It holds that a fair system is one that produces a symmetric seats-votes curve, so that both parties get the same seat shares for any given vote share. The underlying assumption of this approach is that single-member, simple plurality systems cannot be expected to produce proportional outcomes but that they should provide similar outcomes to both major parties. To put it another way, the system should be equal in its disproportionality. If party A gets 25 percent of the seats with 35 percent of the votes, then so should party B. A related concept is responsiveness, which in essence measures the steepness of the seats-votes curve and thus addresses the competitiveness issue. Computing the curve involves some heroic statistical assumptions about what would have happened had the election results been different. Such counterfactual calculations are contestable, to say the least. That, combined with the concept's inherent complexity, was enough to keep it from being widely used or cited in redistricting cases.

The main legal lesson of the second era was that applying the equal protection clause to vote dilution was not as simple as implementing the one-person, one-vote standard. Given that the Court did not want to recognize a right to proportional representation and the standard of total exclusion did not meet the expectations of either the political reform community or voting rights advocates, the effort to stop vote dilution hit a dead end. In the case of partisan vote dilution, the concept was virtually stillborn after the 1981 California congressional redistricting failed to rise above the threshold of constitutional injury. In the case of racial vote dilution, the drift toward rough proportionality proved to be controversial and eventually was limited after *Shaw* v. *Reno*.

Politically, partisan gerrymandering in this period was more prominent than bipartisan deals. The solution to the incumbency advantage in a number of states seemed to be term limits. Starting in the early 1990s, some direct democracy states adopted term limitations for their state legislative seats, partly as a result of the low turnover rates that professionalization seemed to bring. If representatives could be rotated out after a set term, it did not matter whether they negotiated a sweetheart redistricting deal for themselves. California, Colorado, and Oklahoma, which adopted term limits in 1990, were also the first states to undertake redistricting with members who could not aspire to holding the seat indefinitely. That caused members in some cases to be less interested in the design of the seat that they occupied than the one they desired to run for in the future. That in turn destroyed the traditional logroll that those states had developed (that is, the lower and upper houses designed their own district lines and passed each other's lines) and lessened somewhat the idiosyncratic district requests that members would make, since party leaders had to design the seat to be held by someone other than the incumbent later in the decade.

Racial redistricting caused political as well as legal controversy. White liberals fretted with some justification that packing majority-minority seats weakened some of the neighboring white Democratic incumbents and worked to the disadvantage of the Democratic Party as whole.[19] Some Republicans became advocates of majority-minority seats for the same reason. All of that played out against the backdrop of a realigning South, as Southern Republicans gained more representation in Congress and in state legislatures. Even within the protected minority communities, there were those who questioned whether a strict majority-minority redistricting strategy really advanced the political agendas of African Americans and

Hispanics.[20] In short, the quest for ending vote dilution even created some ambivalence within the progressive and reform community.

The Nonfederal Criteria Period (1994 to the present)

The third wave of reform began with the *Shaw* line of cases and the emergence of competition as a redistricting issue. The push for rough proportionality in the 1991 redistricting resulted in some extreme solutions to the underrepresentation of protected groups, particularly in the South, due to widely dispersed African American populations. Fearing that their own efforts would be judged inadequate by the Justice Department, some states drew districts with highly contorted shapes to try to achieve more representation for blacks and Hispanics. The paradigmatic seat was North Carolina's new 12th congressional district in 1991, which was so bizarrely contorted that its image has been reproduced many times in the press and in scholarly publications as an extreme example of affirmative action gerrymandering. Struck down in *Shaw* v. *Reno* (1993) for demonstrating through its shape that the lines had no rational explanation except to separate voters by race, the 12th congressional district marked the end of the aggressive search for racial vote dilution remedies.[21] In *Miller* v. *Johnson* (1995), the Court's emphasis moved somewhat from shape per se to the subordination of traditional redistricting criteria in general.[22] Race could be considered, but it could not be the predominant criterion.

At the beginning of the 2001 round of redistricting, there was much debate about whether the prohibition of race as a predominant redistricting factor would sharply limit the number of majority-minority districts that could and would be drawn. In the end, while the *Shaw* doctrine prevented extreme racial gerrymandering, it did not lead to the dire consequences that many voting rights advocates predicted—because the Court set the threshold for finding race as a predominant factor at a fairly high level (see *Hunt* v. *Cromartie,* 2001) and also because many racially sensitive areas were still covered by section 5 protections against retrogression.[23]

With the limits on preventing vote dilution established, reformers could not expect to ride the Fourteenth Amendment much further. Neither the concept of equal population nor vote dilution prevented incumbents and political parties from redistricting to their mutual benefit. Since the 1960s, there has been a thirty-year period of regional realignment of the political parties, with the South and rural areas trending toward the Republican Party and the Northeast and urban areas to the Democrats. During the course of this transformation, the effects on political competition went largely unnoticed. But when the end of racial realignment coincided with the 2001 round of redistricting, the effects of geographically based districts combined with a racially divided nation were exposed for all to see.

Following the 2001 round, political observers from across the political spectrum, from the editorial pages of the *Washington Post* to those of the *Wall Street Journal*, denounced the power of district boundaries to predetermine election outcomes. The basis of the complaint was that a paltry 10 percent or less of the 2002 and 2004 congressional elections were considered to be competitive by election handicappers. The effective Republican mid-decade redistricting of Texas's congressional districts in 2003 pushed the connection between political boundaries and election outcomes even further into the public spotlight, leaving many to wonder about the health and legitimacy of a House of Representatives based on manipulated boundaries.

Redistricting reform has emerged lately as a proposed method of reinvigorating legislative elections with competition. Since the federal path to redistricting reform has essentially reached a constitutional dead end, the state path seems to be the new frontier. Leading up to and during the apportionment era, seventeen states codified redistricting reform in their constitutions or statutes by removing responsibility for redistricting from a state legislature that was incapable of meeting its obligation to redistrict itself and placing that responsibility in the hands of a redistricting commission.[24] In the 1990s, Alaska, Arizona, and Idaho instituted commissions through popular initiative. These new commissions drew on the existing commission models, such as those of Hawaii and Washington, and on Iowa's unique system, enacted by state statute. At their heart are specific criteria, such as compactness, respect for political subdivisions and communities of interest, incumbent- and partisan-blind provisions, and even provisions for political competitiveness.

Coupled with these criteria-specific reforms was a desire to bring greater transparency to the redistricting process. By 2000, advances in computing technology allowed anyone with a laptop computer and modestly priced software to draw his or her own district, whereas just a decade earlier, only state governments and the political parties could afford the expensive computer systems that redistricting required. Civil rights groups such as MALDEF (Mexican American Legal Defense and Educational Fund) and the NAACP (National Association for the Advancement of Colored People), smaller special interest groups like the Center for Voting and Democracy, and even members of the general public were suddenly able to participate by offering their own plans, and some redistricting authorities actively sought public involvement. The new technology also enabled courts to play a more active role, since they could draw their own maps instead of relying solely on those proposed by opposing litigants in the lawsuits before them.

Some of the more cutting-edge reform efforts in the recent rounds of redistricting focused on nonfederal criteria such as competitiveness and communities of interest. Implementing redistricting criteria other than population equality is anything but straightforward. Even the most fundamental criterion, contiguity, is contestable when bridges and bodies of water or other geographical features connect a district. Compactness may be measured by at least eight different methods that favor some forms over others. A community of interest implies the social and economic similarity of a population, but in exactly what sense? Competitiveness can be observed in elections, but how does one accurately forecast a competitive district? Furthermore, these goals cannot necessarily be achieved simultaneously, along with voting rights concerns; trade-offs must be made. How to weigh one criterion against another is unresolved.

Communities of Interest in Redistricting

Community of interest (COI) considerations are neither universally found in state constitutions nor well defined. The constitutions of only three states, Alaska, Arizona, and Hawaii, specifically mention communities of interest as a redistricting principle. Before 1991, six states mentioned, required, or allowed communities of interest as a districting principle in any form whatsoever, through constitution, statute, or legislative resolutions. Thirteen additional states adopted language that ordered communities of interest to be considered for line drawing in the 1990s. For congressional redistricting specifically, thirteen states required or allowed consideration of communities of interest in 1991 and 2001. Of those, one new state adopted communities of interest in 2001 and one state dropped them. Among the nineteen states that require or encourage the use of communities of interest in congressional or state legislative redistricting, only six have attempted to define what a community of interest is. The definitions range from the very vague "traditional neighborhoods and local communities of interest" (Idaho) to the very specific "ethnic, cultural, economic, trade area, geographic, and demographic factors" (Colorado), but overall there is more ambiguity than certainty in the application and use of this criterion. For states that have no language about COIs in redistricting, the principle can still be justified as generally accepted and used.

While communities of interest as a districting principle had been on the books prior to the most recent redistricting, the warning in *Shaw* against using race as the predominant criterion sent states searching for an alternative to justify majority-minority districts. Communities of interest were a particularly attractive neutral criterion, especially in states with large minority populations, since the vagueness and the lack of a commonly accepted definition allowed creative arguments on what could and should constitute a community of interest. The definition could not come from census data, since the detailed sociodemographic data that might serve as a definition are not released before redistricting must be completed in most states. Consequently, alternative data sources had to be developed by many outside groups and even some states. Alaska, for example, found itself engaged in a full-fledged consultant-conducted study, interviewing hundreds of residents on their commonalities in order to define economic communities of interest. In addition, groups that were not protected under the Voting Rights Act, such as gays and lesbians, also began seeking consideration of their community.

Tying the hands of mapmakers with traditional redistricting principles serves a purpose beyond navigating around the vote dilution potholes. At a basic level, the reforms are designed to prevent gerrymandering. The state constitution or the enabling legislation for redistricting commissions in Alaska, Arizona, Hawaii, and Washington, along with Iowa's codified process, in one way or another prohibit consideration of partisan and incumbent interests in redistricting. Arizona's constitution and Washington's state statutes go a step further by requiring electoral competition.

Declining Competition and Increasing Polarization as a Redistricting Problem

The issue of electoral competition has risen in prominence over the last decade. Congressional election outcomes can be forecast with reasonable accuracy simply by knowing the partisan makeup of a district's population and the party of the incumbent. In the 2002 and 2004 congressional elections, various election handicappers considered 10 percent or less of the 435 House seats competitive—that is, they could not predict the outcome with a high degree of certainty. The small number of competitive districts was unusual; typically incumbents are temporarily vulnerable in the election immediately following a redistricting because they may be detached from their reelection constituency,[25] which prompts the emergence of strategic challengers.[26] Modern incumbent reelection rates to the House average 95 percent. Only seven incumbents were defeated in the 2004 general election, and among those defeats were four members from Texas, who were put at risk by a mid-decade redistricting plan engineered by Representative Tom DeLay (R-Tex.).

Why should we care about competitiveness? On the negative side, competitive seats are more expensive, they often entail the nastiest campaigns, and they can lead candidates to be cautious and ambiguous about what they promise to voters. But in general, political scientists would argue that a democratic system requires some seats to be competitive in order for legislatures to be responsive to electoral change. If the mood or attitudes of voters shift, that should lead to some corresponding change in the share of party- or incumbent-held seats.

In recent years there has been a second argument for competitive seats: namely, that they promote more moderate position taking by representatives. Party polarization in Congress and many state legislatures has been on the rise since the 1980s, and it has reached levels comparable to those in the late nineteenth and early twentieth centuries.[27] No serious academic analyses attribute that polarization solely or even primarily to redistricting. There are many other plausible causes, such as the growing income inequality in the United States, the realignment of the South over civil rights issues, changes in the rules of Congress with respect to the power of its leadership and committees, and the effects of immigration and demographic change. Moreover, there is strong evidence that the polarization trend in the U.S. Senate (which does not redistrict) is almost identical to that in the House (which does)[28] and that the same pattern holds within county and urban and rural units.[29] In short, the partisanship of elected officials is not simply a function of line drawing.

But is legislative polarization even marginally affected by line drawing? There has been no final verdict on that question to date. If one asks the aggregate question, does the sum of all state redistricting equal more safe seats and therefore more partisanship? several reasons could be offered for why the aggregate effects might be unclear. First, since each state controls its own redistricting and since the conditions and processes vary across states, the aggregation of all congressional districts consists of some lines that were drawn in a partisan fashion in some states (for example, Colorado, Texas, and Pennsylvania in the last round), in a bipartisan way in others (California), and in a more neutral way in the remainder (Iowa). Since partisan and bipartisan plans logically lead in different directions,[30] they can neutralize one another to some degree. Partisan plans make the minority party inefficiently safe, whereas bipartisan plans make as many seats of the majority as of the minority party inefficient. In theory, the greater safety of inefficient seats makes their representatives more ideologically polarized, but the partisan (in the case of the majority party seats) and the neutral plans do not. So the net effects of seats moving in different directions in different states might not be as dramatic as one might imagine.

The other point to bear in mind is that inconsistency can be deadly in politics; for fear of being labeled opportunistic or unprincipled, legislators will think long and hard before they reverse their previously held positions. While there is some evidence of increasing polarization over time by sitting members,[31] the most dramatic redistricting effects likely follow replacement, which might happen an election or two after a redistricting.[32] Ironically, displacement of incumbents leading to their replacement is more likely in a partisan than a bipartisan plan.[33]

Still, there is evidence at the individual district level that more competitive seats lead to more moderate members and that "cross-pressured" members are more likely to have more centrist voting scores.[34] Interestingly, apportionment (the reallocation of House seats to states) might have as much or more to do with congressional polarization as redistricting since it has shifted seats into the South and Southwest.[35]

The Effect of Redistricting on Competition

The low level of congressional competition following the 2001 round of redistricting and the partisan re-redistricting in Texas have directed more attention to redistricting in general and led many political observers to speculate that the cause of the decline of competitive congressional *elections* is the decline of competitive congressional *districts* resulting from redistricting. That claim appears in editorial pages across the political spectrum.

To explore the claim, we examined the change of the underlying partisanship of districts before and after redistricting. Various sophisticated statistical methods have been proposed by academics.[36] In practice, mapmakers often evaluate district partisanship by tabulating election information—such as partisan registration, where available, and vote totals for statewide offices—into proposed districts. One measure, which we used

Table 1-1. *Number of Competitive Districts, Normalized Two-Party Presidential Vote*

Competitive range (percent)	1970	1972	1980	1982	1990	1992	2000	2002
45–55	147	150	169	171	153	146	122	111
48–52	52	67	69	79	64	58	53	38

here, is the normalized two-party presidential vote within a district, defined as the Democratic presidential vote divided by the Democratic plus the Republican vote minus the national average of the Democratic and Republican vote. Calculations were made for the most recent presidential election prior to redistricting (for example, for 1990 and 1992, the 1988 presidential election was tabulated for the old and new districts).

Table 1-1 presents the number of competitive districts with a normalized presidential vote within two competitive ranges: a "wide" 45 to 55 percent range and a "narrow" 48 to 52 percent range. The narrow range is nested within the wide range, meaning that districts counted in the narrow range also are counted in the wide range. The table shows that the number of competitive districts actually increased in the 1971 and 1981 rounds of redistricting. However, between 1990 and 1992, the number of competitive districts in the wide range declined by seven districts and by six in the narrow range. Between 2000 and 2002, the number declined by eleven in the wide and by fifteen in the narrow range. Overall, from 1990 to 2002, redistricting was directly responsible for eighteen of forty-two fewer districts in the wide range and for twenty-one of twenty-six districts in the narrow range. On the other hand, a serious decline in the number of competitive seats occurred between redistrictings. From 1990 to 2002, the changes to the underlying political geography of the country were responsible for twenty-four of forty-two fewer competitive districts in the wide range and five of twenty-six in the narrow range.

Why would redistricting result in fewer competitive districts? None of the political actors involved in redistricting favor electoral competition. Incumbents want to get reelected; they would not choose to make the task harder by placing their residence in an unfriendly district. Majority-minority districts often require placing a supermajority of minorities within their borders to guarantee the election of a minority candidate of choice. Since minorities tend to align themselves with the Democrats—or,

Table 1-2. *Number of States Adopting a Bipartisan Gerrymander and Affected Districts*

Unit	1971	1981	1991	2001
States	15	20	19	20
Districts	153	153	147	233

in the case of Cuban Americans, with the Republicans—voting rights districts tend to be some of the most partisan districts. For the political parties, the optimal partisan gerrymander is one that stacks the opposition party in safe districts, thereby wasting its votes on overwhelming victories, and strategically spreads its supporters across the remaining districts, placing just enough opposition voters in the districts to waste their votes in elections they cannot win.[37]

A culprit often cited for the decline in competitive districts is the bipartisan, incumbent-protecting gerrymander. Pitting ambition against ambition might work for the legislative process, but in redistricting it is a recipe for incumbency protection. Incumbents of different parties can make mutual trades of partisans to secure victory in a general election. Forced to work together, the parties may collude to secure the reelection of all their incumbents, resulting in the least competitive of maps. Table 1-2 shows that the number of states enacting bipartisan gerrymanders increased from fifteen to twenty between 1971 and 1981 and has fluctuated between twenty and nineteen since then. Although the number of bipartisan plans increased by only one from 1991 to 2001, the number of districts that were drawn under a bipartisan compromise grew from 147 to 233 due to the adoption of bipartisan plans among larger states, most notably California and Texas. Other large states, such as New York and Ohio, drew bipartisan plans in both 1991 and 2001.

The shift of bipartisan plans from smaller states to larger states has had an important effect on the prospects for drawing competitive districts. Smaller states tend to be politically homogeneous, so it matters little if a partisan, bipartisan, or a neutral map is adopted; redistricting in such states often has only minimal effects on competitiveness. Redistricting is more potent in larger, heterogeneous states whose diverse populations can be strategically grouped for political purposes. California realized a sizable decline in the number of competitive districts between 1991 and 2001, as did Texas, to a lesser extent, before its mid-decade redistricting.

Redistricting institutions vary among the states, with states sometimes having different institutions for congressional and state legislative redistricting.[38] Bipartisan deals emerge under two circumstances. In states that use the legislative process to adopt maps, bipartisan deals may arise when there is divided state government. Among states that use various commissions, some forms of commission are explicitly designed to elicit bipartisan compromise. The growth of bipartisan deals is a result of both an increase in divided governments and the adoption of bipartisan commissions.

A divided government can take one of two forms: a divided legislature or a unified legislature and a governor of a different party. A caveat is that a state government is not truly divided when one party controls a supermajority of the legislature, enabling it to override a governor's veto. A bipartisan compromise congressional plan in a divided government is one that protects incumbents of both parties, where possible, by equalizing populations without weakening the incumbent's partisan base. In state legislative redistricting, such compromises can arise in a divided legislature and result in the respective chambers drawing their own districts. There is always the possibility that a compromise cannot be found, but because redistricting must occur, such situations are resolved in the courts.

Outcomes are listed below for states that used the legislative process for congressional redistricting and had a divided government during redistricting from 1971 to 2001:

—In 1971, fifteen states had a divided government. Ten adopted bipartisan compromises, four went to the courts, and in Tennessee the governor strategically calculated that the Democratic map would give Republicans a chance to win in the partisan gerrymandered districts. Interparty factional bickering led to a bipartisan map in Pennsylvania.

—In 1981, fourteen states had a divided government. Nine adopted bipartisan compromises, and five went to court. Coalitions between wings of different parties arose in Arizona, Nevada, and Washington, resulting in bipartisan maps.

—In 1991, fourteen states had a divided government. Eight adopted bipartisan compromises, and five went to court.

—In 2001, sixteen states had a divided government. Ten adopted bipartisan compromises, and six went to the courts.

Commissions often are cited as the cure to political mischief in redistricting. Bipartisan commissions sometimes are characterized as "nonpartisan" because they force the two parties to work together. These bipartisan institutions are codified into state constitutions and harbinger future bipartisan deals. Generally, two types of commission systems produce bipartisan maps. Commissions in Idaho (adopted 1994), Maine (1964), Missouri (state legislature: house, 1945; senate, 1966), and Washington (1983) must adopt a map by a supermajority vote among an equal number of partisan appointees. Michigan used a similar commission from 1963 to 1982, when it was declared unconstitutional by the state supreme court. Both times that the Michigan commission worked to redistrict congressional districts, the commission stalemated and a court took over. For the other states, commission members are forced to arrive at a bipartisan compromise during the redistricting process, a requirement that resulted in bipartisan maps in every instance of congressional redistricting by these commissions from 1971 through 2001.

Bipartisan compromise occurs at the beginning of the process on commissions in Arizona (adopted 2000), Connecticut (Congress, 1980; state legislature, 1976), and Hawaii (1968). In these states, an equal number of partisan commission members select a tiebreaking member by a supermajority vote, thereby forcing the commission to develop early on a bipartisan compromise in selecting the tiebreaker. Except for Arizona, in all states where such bipartisan commissions operated for congressional redistricting from 1971 through 2001, a bipartisan map was adopted. Arizona is unique in that its commission is composed of citizen members who must follow formal criteria in drawing districts, which weakens the chances of adopting a bipartisan map.

In two of the commission states where bipartisan compromise is institutionalized the legislature also plays a role. Maine's system requires its bipartisan commission to propose maps to the legislature for adoption on a two-thirds vote. Connecticut's procedure calls for the legislature to adopt a map on a supermajority vote, and if that fails, the task falls to the bipartisan commission. For all years that they have operated under their respective systems, these states have adopted bipartisan maps.

The increased use of communities of interest in redistricting, together with improved access to and use of computing technology by "outside" groups, likely had a negative effect on the competitiveness of districts. Communities of interests tend to be politically homogeneous, while competitiveness requires the diversity of opinion that may be found in heterogeneous districts. In a similar manner, competitiveness also is constrained by the need to preserve visible geographic features, along with city, town, and county boundaries (and undivided census tracts), since geographic and political boundaries often coincide with communities of interest. In order to draw competitive districts, large communities of interest must be split and diametrically opposed communities must be grouped together.

Competitiveness is constrained by various redistricting practicalities as well. There are limits to drawing competitive districts in a state that leans toward one of the two major political parties. Competitiveness may be further limited by other goals of redistricting, such as drawing special majority-minority districts and drawing districts that respect communities of interest and existing geographical and political boundaries.

In states that lean toward one party, it is theoretically impossible to draw every district to be competitive. As Niemi and Deegan describe, in creating a competitive district in an uncompetitive state, minority party voters are placed into a district at a level of strength greater than their overall statewide strength.[39] The district that they were taken from will then lean even more toward the dominant party. Eventually, the supply of minority party partisans is exhausted, and the remainder of the state must be composed of uncompetitive districts for the dominant party. Drawing for competitiveness in a partisan leaning state politically favors the minority party; it is, in its own way, a partisan gerrymander.

Opportunities for drawing competitive districts may also be affected by drawing special minority-majority districts to comply with the Voting Rights Act. Majority-minority districts concentrate minority populations, and since nonwhite groups (except for Cuban Americans in southern Florida) tend heavily to vote Democratic, majority-minority districts tend to be uncompetitive Democratic districts. That tendency is further exacerbated by the fact that nonminorities and minorities living in minority communities often come from similar socioeconomic backgrounds, which favors minority and Democratic candidates. If Democrats are the dominant statewide political party, majority-minority districts (depending on how many will be drawn) will be consistent with the goal of competitiveness, since drawing majority-minority districts would balance the residual pool of voters in a more competitive direction. If Republicans are the dominant political party, drawing minority-majority districts will reduce the opportunities to draw competitive districts by placing already "scarce" Democrats into uncompetitive minority-majority districts.

One way to promote the creation of competitive districts is to mandate it through law. Two states, Arizona and Washington, have competitiveness clauses requiring their commissions to draw districts to favor competitiveness. These states, along with Iowa, provide examples of the types of redistricting institutions that may foster the creation of competitive districts.

In Washington, a bipartisan commission meets behind closed doors to conduct redistricting. Bipartisan deals that are brokered between the parties are not challenged in court since usually only the political parties have the monetary muscle to enjoin lawsuits. Thus, while it is in state statute, Washington's competitiveness clause is largely unenforced.

In Arizona, a citizen redistricting commission was established by initiative in 2000. Proposition 106 stipulates six criteria for the commission to follow in formulating a new districting plan. The first five criteria deal with traditional redistricting goals such as equal population, respect for the Voting Rights Act, ignorance of incumbent residence, and respect for communities of interest and existing political boundaries. The sixth requirement is that "[t]o the extent practicable, competitive districts should be favored where to do so would create no significant detriment to the other goals." Unlike those on Washington's commission, the members of the Arizona commission are citizens who have limited ties to government and the political parties. The tiebreaking member on the commission must not be registered as a member of a major party. Together, those factors favor the creation of more competitive districts than those in Washington.

Iowa often is referred to as a "commission state" because a nonpartisan legislative support group called the Legislative Service Agency (LSA), formerly the Legislative Service Bureau, proposes maps to the legislature for its approval. In this respect, the Iowa commission is modeled on civil service boundary commissions in other countries, where career bureaucrats, not politicians, draw district boundaries. However, Iowa's system exists only under state statute, and the legislature can assume redistricting authority under the statute as well as amend the statute.[40]

Iowa's process often is placed on a pedestal because it consistently produces competitive districts. Currently, four of the five are widely considered competitive. However, the districts would likely be competitive even if incumbent or partisan interests drew them. Furthermore, Iowa's system is not a panacea for the problem of politics in redistricting. Although the LSA cannot consider political data when drawing maps, the legislature can and does. According to *Congressional Quarterly Weekly*, when Republicans controlled the state government in 1981, the legislature approved a map on the third attempt, after rejecting two previous maps that would have had a negative impact on the reelection of two incumbent Republicans.

The lesson from these states is that two tactics play a role in creating competitive districts. One is limiting the role of partisans in redistricting and the other is limiting the role of incumbents. Incumbent interests can be limited by deleting information about the location of incumbents' homes. Partisan interests can be minimized by removing overt partisans from the redistricting process, through a citizen commission, as in Arizona, or nonpartisan legislative support staff, as in Iowa. Given highly partisan legislative support staff in other states, the import of the Iowa model may not be ideal for all states.

It would also seem to be sensible to include favoring competitiveness on any list of criteria if the goal is to create competitive districts. But election results are needed to evaluate the competitiveness of districts, and they also are needed to evaluate the impact of redistricting on the Voting Rights Act (VRA). Since Iowa has few, if any, VRA compliance problems, it can ignore political data, but states with significant minority populations can ill afford to follow Iowa's example.

Conclusion

Most of the redistricting reforms in the post–World War II period were driven by the logic of the Constitution's equal protection clause. Vote dilution doctrine seems at this point to have gone as far as the Court will allow it. Moreover, the new problem, noncompetitive districts, seems ill fitted for a rights framework. That means that reform will have to rely on state constitutional and statutory provisions or institutional arrangements such as redistricting commissions. It will not be easy to define competition by a bright-line test, and many institutional arrangements that accommodate competing parties (whether citizens or elected officials) tend to reduce rather than increase the number of competitive seats.

Notes

1. *Baker* v. *Carr*, 369 U.S. 186 (1962).
2. *Colegrove* v. *Green*, 328 U.S. 549 (1946).
3. Melissa Cully Anderson, "Venturing onto the Path of Equal Representation," in *Earl Warren and the Warren Court: The Legacy in American and Foreign Law—A Half-Century Perspective*, edited by Harry Scheiber (Berkeley, Calif.: IGS Press, forthcoming).
4. *Wesberry* v. *Sanders*, 376 U.S. 1 (1964); *Reynolds* v. *Sims*, 377 U.S. 533 (1964); and *Avery* v. *Midland County*, 390 U.S. 474 (1968).
5. *Abate* v. *Mundt*, 403 U.S 182 (1971); *Mahan* v. *Howell*, 410 U.S. 315 (1973); *Brown* v. *Thomson*, 462 U.S. 835 (1983); *Voinovich* v. *Quilter*, 507 U.S 146 (1993).

6. *Swann* v. *Adams*, 385 U.S. 440 (1967); *Kirkpatrick* v. *Preisler*, 394 U.S. 526 (1969); and *White* v. *Weiser*, 412 U.S. 783 (1973).

7. Gary Cox and Jonathon Katz, *Elbridge Gerry's Salamander* (Cambridge University Press, 2002).

8. Timothy O'Rourke, *The Impact of Reapportionment* (New Brunswick, N.J.: Transaction Books, 1980).

9. Mathew D. McCubbins and Thomas Schwartz, "Politics, the Courts, and Public Policy: Consequences of the One Man, One Vote Rule," *American Journal of Political Science* 32 (May 1988): 388–415; Stephen Ansolabehere, Alan Gerber, and James M. Snyder Jr., "Equal Votes, Equal Money: Court-Ordered Redistricting and the Distribution of Public Expenditures in the American States," *American Political Science Review* 96 (December 2002): 767–78.

10. *Burns* v. *Richardson*, 384 U.S. 73 (1966).

11. *Karcher* v. *Daggett*, 462 U.S. 725 (1983).

12. *Gaffney* v. *Cummings*, 412 U.S. 735 (1973).

13. *Mobile* v. *Bolden*, 446 U.S. 55 (1980); and *White* v. *Regester*, 412 U.S. 755 (1973).

14. Douglas Rae, *The Political Consequences of Electoral Laws* (Yale University Press, 1971).

15. Arend Lijphart, *Patterns of Democracy: Government Forms and Performance in Thirty-Six Countries* (Yale University Press, 1999).

16. *Davis* v. *Bandemer*, 478 U.S. 109 (1986).

17. The Bandemer standard was successfully invoked once in *Republican Party of North Carolina* v. *Martin*, 980 F.2d 943 (4th Cir. 1993), a case involving at-large judicial elections in North Carolina in which the court found that at-large elections in the state were intended to deny the election of Republicans.

18. *Thornburg* v. *Gingles*, 478 U.S. 30 (1986).

19. David Lublin, *The Paradox of Representation: Racial Gerrymandering and Minority Interests in Congress* (Princeton University Press, 1997).

20. Carol Swain, *Black Faces, Black Interests: The Representation of African-Americans in Congress* (Harvard University Press, 1993).

21. *Shaw* v. *Reno*, 509 U.S. 630 (1993).

22. *Miller* v. *Johnson*, 515 U.S. 900 (1995).

23. *Hunt* v. *Cromartie*, 532 U.S. 121 (2001).

24. Michael P. McDonald, "A Comparative Analysis of U.S. State Redistricting Institutions," *State Politics and Policy Quarterly* 4, no. 4 (2004): 371–96.

25. Stephen Ansolabehere, James M. Snyder Jr., and Charles Stewart III, "Old Voters, New Voters, and the Personal Vote: Using Redistricting to Measure the Incumbency Advantage," *American Journal of Political Science* 44, no. 1 (2000): 17–34; Scott W. Desposato and John R Petrocik, "The Variable Incumbency Advantage: New Voters, Redistricting, and the Personal Vote," *American Journal of Political Science* 47, no. 1 (2003): 18–22.

26. Marc J. Hetherington, Bruce A. Larson, and Suzanne Globetti, "The Redistricting Cycle and Strategic Candidate Decisions in U.S. House Races," *Journal of Politics* 65, no. 4 (2003): 1221–35.

27. Gary C. Jacobson, "Explaining the Ideological Polarization of the Congressional Parties since the 1970s," paper presented at the Annual Meeting of the Midwest Political Science Association, Chicago, April 15, 2004; David Brady and Hahrie Han, "An Extended Historical View of Congressional Party Polarization," paper presented at Princeton University, December 2, 2004; Nolan McCarty, Keith Poole, and Howard Rosenthal, "Polarized America: The Dance of Ideology and Unequal Riches," Center on Institutions and Governance Working Paper 5, Institute of Governmental Studies, University of California, Berkeley (February 2005).

28. McCarty, Poole, and Rosenthal, "Polarized America," p. 40; Brady and Han, "An Extended Historical View of Congressional Party Polarization," p. 8.

29. David Hopkins, "Geographic Polarization in American Presidential Elections," paper presented at the Annual Meeting of the Midwest Political Science Association, Chicago, April 7, 2005.

30. Bruce E. Cain, *The Reapportionment Puzzle* (University of California Press, 1984).

31. Jacobson, "Explaining the Ideological Polarization of the Congressional Parties," p. 20.

32. Brady and Han, "An Extended Historical View of Congressional Party Polarization," p. 24.

33. Cain, *The Reapportionment Puzzle*; McCarty, Poole, and Rosenthal, "Polarized America."

34. Brady and Han, "An Extended Historical View of Congressional Party Polarization," p. 21.

35. McCarty, Poole, and Rosenthal, "Polarized America," p. 43.

36. Andrew Gelman and Gary King, "A Unified Method of Evaluating Electoral Systems and Redistricting Plans," *American Journal of Political Science* 38, no. 2 (1994): 514–54.

37. Cain, *The Reapportionment Puzzle*.

38. McDonald, "A Comparative Analysis of U.S. State Redistricting Institutions."

39. Richard G. Niemi and John Deegan Jr., "A Theory of Political Districting," *American Political Science Review* 72, no. 4 (1978): 1304–23.

40. The LSA proposes a sequence of three maps to the legislature, any of which may be adopted by majority vote. The first two maps may only be amended for technical reasons; however, the third map may be amended within the full context of the normal legislative process. It is here that the legislature may invoke its authority. However, in the history of this convoluted process, adopted in 1970, the legislature has never rejected a third proposal from the LSA, fearing that to do otherwise would invite the perception of partisan politics at play in the process. For this reason, too, perhaps, the legislature has not amended the state statute governing the process.

2 The Impact of Redistricting on Candidate Emergence

L. Sandy Maisel, Cherie D. Maestas, and Walter J. Stone

The problem has become so familiar that it hardly bears repeating, but it is so fundamental to American democracy that it must be repeated.[1] Competition in congressional elections—at the district level—has all but disappeared. To be sure, the two major parties compete fiercely for control of the House. But though the Republicans have only a thirty-seat advantage in the House today, few experts give the Democrats much chance of winning the sixteen seats needed to reclaim control in 2006.

A sixteen-seat swing in a congressional election is not unheard of. During the 1970s and 1980s, swings of that magnitude were quite common, but in the last ten elections, that number has been reached only once, when the Republicans won by a landslide in 1994. In the last five elections, the partisan swing has been between three and eight seats.[2]

The authors would like to thank Sarah Fulton, at the University of California, Davis, for help in preparing the data for this analysis and Andrea Berchowitz and Claire Walsh, at Colby College, for assistance in manuscript preparation. The 2002 wave of the Candidate Emergence Study was funded by a grant from the Carnegie Corporation of New York, for whose support we are most grateful. The Carnegie Corporation, of course, bears no responsibility for the views presented in this chapter.

Not only do few seats change partisan hands, but few races are close. In recent elections as many as 90 percent of incumbents seeking reelection have won by margins of more than 10 percent; of those, half have won by margins of 30 percent or more. Nearly 15 percent of those seeking seats in the House faced no major party opposition. More than 42 percent of the incumbents seeking reelection in 2004 (172 of 401) won by margins of more than 40 percent. And that lack of competition on election day hardly came as a surprise. Various organizations that monitor congressional elections, such as the *Cook Political Report*, the *Rothenberg Political Report*, and Congressional Quarterly's *Politics Today*, regularly rate races as being safe for one party or the other, leaning one way or the other, or having no clear favorite. In the last two election cycles, those analysts have rated less than 10 percent of the seats as being in play. With nearly perfect accuracy, they have been able to predict the winners in approximately 90 percent of the races—not only before the votes are cast, but often many months before.

In a joint appearance in spring 2005, a year before the casting of the first primary vote for the 2006 congressional elections, Stu Rothenberg, editor and publisher of the *Rothenberg Political Report,* and Amy Walter, House of Representatives editor for the *Cook Political Report,* agreed that fewer than thirty seats will be in play during those elections. Both agreed that as the 2006 elections approach, the number of districts that will be truly competitive will be less than half of that.[3] *Politics Today* claims that there are only twenty-nine seats in which one candidate or the other is not clearly favored.[4]

Redistricting is a central part of the story of the lack of competition. The turmoil that occurred in Texas in 2003, for example, illustrates how redistricting shapes competition. Depending on whose view one subscribes to, Texas's thirty-two districts were redrawn either to benefit the Republican Party or to redress the gerrymandering that had favored the Democrats two years earlier. The goal of legislators and the governor was to concentrate Democrats in as few seats as possible, put Anglo Democrats into seats that they would have difficulty holding, and create solidly Republican districts.[5] The effort was remarkably successful: only one of the targeted Democrats, Chet Edwards, in the Waco–College Station central Texas seat, survived. More to the point, as analysts look to 2006, thirty-one of the thirty-two seats are seen as solidly under one party's control or the other— twenty-one favoring the Republicans and ten the Democrats, with only Edwards's seat in doubt. That seat would be solidly Republican if the incumbent were not a Democrat.

What do changes such as these mean for the quality of representation in Texas, or in any other state? It is very clear that when redistricting is used to benefit one party, competition decreases in many districts. But more important, when competition decreases, fewer strong potential candidates are willing to step into the ring and citizens' choices are thereby reduced.

The Impact of Redistricting on the Supply of Strong Candidates

Our concern is less with the impact of redistricting on incumbent or party advantage and more with the impact on competition itself, the topic that originally drew political scientist Edward Tufte's interest.[6] Redistricting, particularly as practiced in the most recent election cycle, contributes to a drop in competition in congressional elections—and presumably in state legislative elections as well. We are concerned here with one particular aspect of the impact of redistricting on competition: the role that it has played in candidate emergence.

In conceptualizing the problem, we have purposely chosen the term "candidate emergence" rather than "candidate recruitment." There is ample evidence that national parties as well as state and local parties are heavily involved in recruiting candidates for federal office.[7] But there also is ample evidence that potential candidates consider many factors in addition to party recruitment efforts and that party leaders do very little recruiting at all in many districts.[8] Candidate emergence implies a process that is much broader than recruitment by parties or by any of a number of other political actors; it also includes the strategic choices of potential candidates as they consider a variety of personal and political factors in deciding whether to run.

Our concern is that redistricting and the partisan nature of the procedures used to redraw boundaries in some states might decrease the chances that strong challengers from one of the two major parties will emerge. Potential candidates for office are aware of the many tools available to political gerrymanderers and understand the skill with which they use those tools. Consequently, potential candidates' impressions of the ways in which those tools and skills will be used can deter them from running for office.

Because the redistricting in Texas in 2003 was done with such an open political agenda, it is instructive to review it to see how redistricting might affect candidate emergence. In some cases, the party favored by the redistricting process might gain candidates. Three districts in Texas held by Democrats (districts 1, 2, and 17) were drawn to increase the chances of a

Republican victory. As a result, far more than the normal number of Republican candidates entered the primary to run against the Democratic incumbent because winning that nomination was seen to have more political value than winning an ordinary nomination to run against an incumbent. In two of those districts, six candidates filed in the Republican primary; in the other, three.[9] However, in many more cases, potential candidates expected less than favorable outcomes from redistricting, and those expectations decreased their willingness to run. In seven other districts, no candidates emerged to run against incumbents, even though some were recruited. The nominations were not seen as valuable, or, at least, they were not seen as valuable enough to give up whatever a potential candidate might have to sacrifice to run.[10]

It is easy to imagine that the redistricting battle that dominated the Texas political scene for months might well have had an impact on candidate emergence. Undoubtedly, potential candidates watched carefully as the lines were drawn to see how their futures might be affected. But what about potential candidates in other states? According to the *Cook Political Report*, Texas was not unique:

> Another trouble spot for the Democrats is the spotty nature of their recruiting efforts. Republican freshman incumbents who won close races in 2002, or who sit in marginal districts, . . . lack serious (or in some cases any) Democratic opponents. Democrats were unable to get their first (or second, or third for that matter) choice in the open PA-15 seat. . . . To be fair, Republicans have not exactly run the table on recruiting either. . . . Republicans have also seen some of their top-flight candidates say no.[11]

Although we do not know the extent to which redistricting played a role in strong potential candidates' decisions to resist party recruitment efforts, we do believe that the lack of strong candidates is a problem and that it is worthwhile to determine the extent to which redistricting plays a role in their decisions not to run.

The Candidate Emergence Study

To explore how potential candidates for the House of Representatives view the process of redistricting and the expected outcomes, we used data from a survey of strong potential candidates for office in more than 150 districts across the nation. The Candidate Emergence Study began in 1997 with two goals in mind: first, as a purely academic study, to explore decision-making by those who might seek to run for the U.S. House of Representatives; and second, to determine whether there were structural elements in the electoral process that systematically worked to deter competition. We took as our starting point the premise that high-quality candidates for office serve democracy better by allowing for the discussion of policy alternatives and that the weakness of candidates for the House of Representatives in many districts, defined as their inability to reach voters with their message, is a weakness in the U.S. representative system of government. None of the redistricting experiences since 1998 has led us to think that the project is any less important. Too many House races feature no real competition; too many incumbents either are not challenged or are challenged by candidates who cannot get their message to the voters, who cannot force a real discussion of the issues. Our goal was not to encourage particular candidates to run for office but to determine whether qualified candidates existed in districts in which none were running and, if so, to ascertain why some individuals ran for office and others did not.[12]

In this chapter we draw on data from surveys of potential candidates for office in 2002 to assess the impact of redistricting as a deterrent to the emergence of strong potential candidates (PCs).[13] Our potential candidate pool was made up of PCs whose names were recommended to us by a sample of political informants, of political party elites and community leaders from each party in each district, and of all state legislators whose districts overlap with the congressional districts in which we are exploring potential candidate decisionmaking. In 2002, we also drew potential candidates from published web sources, and we permitted our political informants to designate themselves as potential candidates. We mailed to 4,562 PCs (after adjusting for bad addresses) and received 1,537 responses, a response rate of 33.5 percent.[14] More than half of our respondents (58 percent) expressed an attraction to a career in the U.S. House. They were precisely the type of individuals that we wished to study to understand the effects of redistricting—politically involved citizens and officeholders, many harboring some ambition for a House seat.[15]

The 2002 survey included specific questions about redistricting so that we could better understand how the redistricting process and outcomes affected potential candidates' perceptions of their districts, their chances of winning, and ultimately their interest in running. We asked potential candidates to estimate the effects of redistricting on the composition of their

U.S. House district and on the prospects for candidates from each party. Because some states were still in the process of redistricting at the time of the survey, we also asked respondents how certain they were about the district changes. Just over 1,300 respondents resided in states where redistricting was in progress or recently had been completed, and 55 percent of them expressed some uncertainty over district boundaries. Finally, we asked potential candidates to indicate whether the uncertainty surrounding redistricting discouraged them from running for the House. These data form the core of our analysis and allowed us to explore how ambitious potential candidates view the redistricting process during the time that they are considering whether to run for the House.

The Impact of Redistricting on Potential Candidates

Potential candidates varied a great deal in terms of how they viewed the redistricting process. Their views were subjective and based at least in part on partisan differences (see table 2-1). Those who identified themselves as Republicans tended to see district changes as favoring Republicans, while those who identified themselves as Democrats saw the changes as favoring Democrats.

However, their perceptions were based on much more than partisanship. Within partisan categories, there was variation at the state, district, and individual levels. Respondents in different states—which presumably had different political histories and different redistricting processes—viewed the process differently. Beyond that, there was variation among the perceptions of respondents from different districts within the same state and even among individual respondents from the same district.

By changing district lines, the redistricting process creates uncertainty, taking some voters out of a district and bringing new voters in. The actual impact of the changes cannot be known in concrete detail until after an election is held. However, PCs' perceptions of the effect of the changes were important when PCs were deciding whether to run. Some PCs were more optimistic than others about the impact that the same changes were likely to have on their electoral prospects in a district. And their decisions, we hold, were based on overly optimistic perceptions.

Our data do show, however, that PCs based their perceptions in part at least on the process used in their state. Each state varies in the type of redistricting process used, but for U.S. House districts most states use a process

Table 2-1. *Potential Candidate's View of the Effect of Boundary Changes in Home District*
Percent

Effect	All respondents	Republican respondents	Democratic respondents
Favors Republicans	43	53	34
Toss-up	28	30	27
Favors Democrats	29	17	39
Number of cases	1,123	525	596

Source: Candidate Emergence Study Survey, 2002.

that begins in the legislature and ends with a gubernatorial signature or veto.[16] That makes the process inherently political and creates a set of cues, or expectations, about its outcome, and those expectations are central to the candidate emergence process. When considering a run for office, potential candidates carefully weigh their chances of winning, and the location of district boundaries is an important determinant of their chances. It is therefore vital to understand how the *process* of redistricting creates such expectations.

Table 2-2 shows that PCs viewed the process differently depending on both partisan control of the legislature and type of redistricting process used. We compared states that use a legislative process with those that have a commission, or nonpartisan, process. We also included in the latter category states in which the redistricting fight moved into the court system before or during the period of our survey.

The table clearly shows that the expectation of partisan effects was stronger among potential candidates in states where the process was controlled by a partisan legislature than in states where redistricting was controlled by a commission or the courts.[17] For example, 68.8 percent of PCs in states in which a Republican legislature controlled the redistricting process saw boundary changes as helping Republicans, while only 45.7 percent held that view when the process was controlled by the courts or a commission. PCs expected Democrats to fare much worse in Republican-controlled states when the process was controlled by the legislature. Only 16 percent believed that changes in their district would favor Democrats in states redistricted by the legislature, while 27.2 percent of those in states with a nonpartisan redistricting process saw Democrats as gaining ground in their district.[18]

Table 2-2. *Potential Candidates' View of Redistricting Effect by Type of Process and Government*
Percent

Effect	Unified (Republican)	Divided (Republican legislature/ Democratic governor)	Divided (split chambers)	Divided (Democratic legislature/ Republican governor)	Unified (Democrat)
			Type of government		
Legislative process					
Favors Republicans	68.8	48.7	37.9	15.6	32.3
Toss-up	15.3	42.3	30.5	46.9	21.6
Favors Democrats	16.0	9.0	31.6	37.5	46.1
Number of cases	282	78	95	128	167
Commission or court process					
Favors Republicans	45.7	33.3	37.3	36.7	23.3
Toss-up	27.2	33.3	34.0	35.0	23.3
Favors Democrats	27.2	33.3	28.8	28.3	53.5
Number of cases	81	36	153	60	43

Source: Candidate Emergence Study Survey, 2002.

It also is notable that a divided government reduced the expectation of partisan bias in redistricting. When redistricting plans by the legislature were subject to veto by a governor of the opposition party, fewer potential candidates expected a partisan outcome. Sixty-nine percent of potential candidates in unified Republican states expected Republican-favoring outcomes; in contrast, only 48.7 percent did so in Republican states with a Democrat as governor. A similar difference is apparent between potential candidates in unified Democratic states and those in states with a Democratic legislature and Republican governor. Moreover, the number of potential candidates who viewed the outcome as a "toss-up" grew dramatically when government control is split between the parties.

These results highlight a very important and often overlooked fact: procedures interact with political context to influence the expectations of prospective challengers. The first election cycle following redistricting is the most difficult for potential candidates to assess because they have no evidence on which to base their expectations. Although in later cycles they can rely on past election data to help identify opportunities, newly drawn districts can be unpredictable. Indeed, some potential candidates must make the decision to commit to a race before boundaries are settled. In both cases, the procedures used in each state become an important source of information to potential candidates about how district changes might affect their fortunes.

Certainly, estimating how redistricting affects the electoral fortunes of incumbents is a central part of the decisionmaking process. PCs are more likely to run if they see the incumbent as having been hurt by redistricting, less likely if the incumbent appears to have been favored. Table 2-3 shows that the partisan processes associated with redistricting shaped their views as well. Here, we examined only potential candidates in states where the legislature controlled redistricting.

Table 2-3 demonstrates that in states in which the redistricting process was partisan, PCs clearly expected the effects of new district boundaries in districts with Democratic House incumbents to differ from those in districts with Republican House incumbents. Only 7 percent of PCs in Republican-held House districts believed that boundary changes would favor challengers, while 60 percent of PCs in Democratic-held House districts did; similarly, 75 percent of the former expected redistricting to favor incumbent Republicans, while only 27 percent of the latter expected it to favor incumbent Democrats.[19]

While the magnitude of difference is smaller in Democratic states, the pattern is identical: PCs expected the party controlling the legislature to reward its own incumbents. Although this finding is not surprising, the implications should not be overlooked. Partisan redistricting processes create a set of expectations about outcomes, and those expectations condition a PC's decision to run in important ways.

Perhaps most important is how expectations affected potential candidates' estimates of the incumbents' chances of winning. The survey asked potential candidates to estimate the chances that an incumbent would win the nomination if he or she sought it and win the general election if he or she won the nomination. Chances were ranked from *extremely unlikely* through *toss up* to *extremely likely*. We scored the items on a seven-point subjective probability scale to make the results easy to interpret.[20]

Not surprisingly, the average estimate of incumbent chances is quite high: .79. However, the estimate of incumbent chances is .85 for districts in which PCs expected boundary changes to favor the incumbent party, while it is .71 for districts in which they expected changes to favor challengers. The difference is both statistically significant ($p < .05$) and substantively

Table 2-3. *Potential Candidate's View of Incumbent Protection Effect of Redistricting by Incumbent's Party and Type of Government*
Percent

Effect by type of government	Party of incumbent in PC's home district	
	Republican	Democrat
Unified Republican		
Favors challenger's party	7.1	60.3
Toss-up	17.4	12.4
Favors incumbent's party	75.5	27.3
Number of cases	155	121
Divided government[a]		
Favors challenger's party	17.3	15.7
Toss-up	40.5	40.5
Favors incumbent's party	42.2	43.8
Number of cases	173	121
Unified Democratic		
Favors challenger's party	26.7	15.5
Toss-up	24.4	19.7
Favors incumbent's party	48.8	64.8
Number of cases	86	71

Source: Candidate Emergence Study Survey, 2002.
a. Either the governor and control of the legislature belong to different parties or the legislature is split between two parties.

significant. As we show below, incumbent chances figure heavily into potential candidates' estimates of their own chances of winning.

Potential candidates are strategic politicians.[21] Whether they think that they can win is one important factor in deciding whether to run. Table 2-4 explores how changes in district boundaries affected potential candidates' perceptions of their chances of winning. Here, we used a dichotomous measure to indicate whether the changes in district boundaries were seen as favorable to candidates from the PC's party. We measured chances of winning by asking the chances that the PC would win the nomination if he or she chose to run in 2002 and the chances that the PC would win the general election if he or she won the nomination. We used the same seven-point answer scale described above, rescaled as a pseudo-probability.

Table 2-4. *Potential Candidate's View of Redistricting Effect and of Personal Chances of Winning*

Effect	Nomination chance	General election chance	Overall chances
Favors challenger's party	0.43	0.30	0.17
Favors PC's party	0.28	0.57	0.19

Source: Candidate Emergence Study Survey, 2002.

We found that district boundaries had opposite effects on PCs' assessment of their chances of winning the nomination and of winning the general election.[22] When boundary changes were seen as favoring the opposite party, the measure of the chances of winning the nomination is higher. When boundary changes were seen as favoring the PC's party, the measure of the chances of winning the nomination is .15 lower. The opposite occurs at the general election stage. While potential candidates saw their chances as going up in the general election stage, they saw them as going down in the nomination stage, because PCs expected stronger intraparty competition for the nomination. However, they believed that once the nomination was secured, the chances of winning the general election were much higher. Candidates from the party that was not seen as favored by the redistricting process saw themselves as more likely to win the nomination because the nomination was less valuable and fewer people would seek the nomination since their general election chances would be lower.

To get a better idea of how PCs viewed the effects of boundary changes on their overall chances of winning the seat, we ran a multivariate ordinary least squares (OLS) model using joint chances of winning the nomination and the general election (overall chances of winning the seat) as our dependent variable (table 2-5). We controlled for several key factors, such as the party of the potential candidate relative to that of the incumbent, the quality of the potential candidate, the prospects of the incumbent, and whether the seat was open or in a safe district.[23] Even after controlling for those factors, we still saw a positive, significant effect of redistricting. Potential candidates who viewed boundary changes as favorable to their own party viewed their chances as somewhat higher. Of course, the overall effects are larger than those represented by the coefficient because redistricting works indirectly through influencing incumbents' chances as well. However, we

Table 2-5. *Potential Candidate's Chances of Winning*[a]

Variable	β (SE)	Significance
Redistricting favors PC's party	.0086 (.004)	**
PC's strength as a campaigner	.046 (.006)	***
PC named in media as prospective challenger	.107 (.017)	***
PC and incumbent of same party	−.028 (.017)	**
PC's assessment of incumbent's chances	−.082 (.028)	***
Open seat	.060 (.024)	***
Noncompetitive district balance	−.023 (.015)	*
Constant	−.052 (.064)	
Summary statistic		
Number of cases	805	
$F(7, 534)$	21.6***	***
Adjusted R^2	.152	

Source: Candidate Emergence Study Survey, 2002.
a. Ordinary least squares regression; *** p<.01; **p <.05; *p<.10, one-tailed tests.

also note in table 2-5 that a district with a noncompetitive partisan balance has a negative effect on the chances of winning. That reflects the fact that PCs understood that they had to clear two hurdles—a primary and a general election—in order to secure a seat in the House and that the chance of clearing both is easier in a competitive district than in one with a partisan imbalance, even if that imbalance favors their party.

The effects of redistricting on chances of winning are important because chances of winning are closely related to our principle concern, a potential candidate's decision on whether to run (table 2-6). On average, potential candidates who assessed their chances of winning as less than 1 in 5 were very unlikely to run while those who assessed their chances as better than fifty-fifty were nine times more likely to run. We found that redistricting works indirectly to discourage PCs from running by reducing their per-

Table 2-6. *Potential Candidate's Chances of Running by Chances of Winning*

Chances of winning	Chances of running
Less than .20	.04
Number of cases	502
Between .20 and .50	.16
Number of cases	150
Greater than .5	.36
Number of cases	86

Source: Candidate Emergence Study Survey, 2002.

ception of their chance of success. Boundary change affects the perceived competitive context and thus potential candidate decisionmaking.

Finally, redistricting introduces a great deal of uncertainty into the strategic calculus. Although we show that PCs form expectations about the outcome of redistricting based on the redistricting process, the degree to which they are certain about those changes remains important. Table 2-7 shows another way in which redistricting discourages potential candidates. Politicians want to know the rules of the game before they enter a contest. Table 2-7 demonstrates that many of the PCs who we surveyed were uncertain about the changes that redistricting would work on their districts and even more so if they feared that redistricting would favor the opposition party; however, they experienced a significant degree of uncertainty no matter what their expectations. Uncertainty itself deters candidacy, as it is

Table 2-7. *Potential Candidates Who Feel Discouraged from Running by Redistricting Effect*
Percent

PC's degree of certainty about effect	Potential candidate's view of redistricting effect		
	Favors PC's party	*Favors neither party*	*Favors opposition party*
Pretty certain or certain	17.0	11.0	25.0
Uncertain	31.0	43.0	46.0

Source: Candidate Emergence Study Survey, 2002.

unlikely that a candidate will go into a race without some clear sense of what the district will look like.[24]

Conclusions

If lack of competition in House elections is a concern, it is important to understand how strong potential candidates for House seats decide whether to seek election. We felt from the beginning that we had a good understanding of the factors that enter into potential candidates' decision-making, but we did not know the ways in which those factors—personal and strategic considerations—worked to influence potential candidates' decisions. We also did not know whether structural aspects of the electoral process could be altered to improve the chances that better-qualified candidates would run for office. Finally, while all of us working on this project have agreed from the beginning that better-qualified candidates would run better campaigns, we were less certain whether better campaigns, while valuable in their own right, would necessarily lead to more competition.

The process of redistricting is one of the few aspects of the electoral environment that can be changed, in this case through legislation at the state level. We viewed the effect of the process through the lens of potential candidates, for their decisions determine the supply of candidates who run for the House. If potential candidates see redistricting as a deterrent, then changes in redistricting rules could increase the supply of strong candidates, including challengers of incumbents.

A caveat is in order. Any change in the redistricting process would have an impact only in some states, some of the time. Clearly, states with only one congressional district do not have to worry about the redistricting process. States with a small number of districts that do not change after reapportionment generally see only minor changes in district boundaries.[25] Similarly, states with limited population movement see limited change.[26] The process of redistricting has the most potential impact in states that gain or lose seats as a result of reapportionment and in states with significant shifts in population. These factors must be kept in mind in reviewing our conclusions. In fact, our findings are understated for potential candidates in states in which significant redistricting occurs, because potential candidates in states with little redistricting surely would have replied that the process had little or no effect on their perceptions of the district, their perceptions of their chances of winning, or their degree of certainty about the makeup of the district.

With that stated, our findings point to the importance of the redistricting process in the minds of potential candidates. First, potential candidates view redistricting as what it is in most states, a quintessentially political process. Parties that control redistricting try to draw districts that favor their party; potential candidates understand that. This finding is particularly true for states in which the legislature controls the redistricting process and Republicans control the legislature, but it holds to a lesser degree in states where redistricting is controlled by Democrats and even, in terms of perceptions, in states in which neither party controls the process.

Further, we note that PCs saw redistricting as favoring incumbents of the party that controlled the legislature. Considering the number of states in which redistricting has only a minor impact because of the number of seats involved, the extent to which this finding holds is impressive. Our PCs generally saw their districts as leaning heavily toward one party or the other, a perception that is essentially an evaluation of the impact of previous efforts at redistricting. As a result, candidates of the party in power saw that achieving victory in a primary would be difficult, while PCs in the minority party saw that although they might have an easy time gaining a nomination, winning a general election would be much harder.[27] That is to say, PCs saw their chances of winning as best in tightly competitive districts—more so even than in districts favoring their own party—and past redistricting, in areas where it can play such a role, has led to the existence of few competitive districts.

When looking at current redistricting, PCs saw the process as hindering their chances of winning. They were discouraged to run by many factors, including the uncertainties created by redistricting. Their discouragement worked in at least two ways. First, they assumed that the change, whether it helped their party or not, was going to create an environment that was less competitive in a partisan sense. That would hurt their chances of winning whether they were in the majority party (and would have to run either against an incumbent or, if the seat was open, against a strong field of challengers who assume that the winner of the primary will win the general election) or the minority party (and they would likely lose a general election even if they won the nomination easily). Second, they were uncertain about the specific political effects of the redistricting, certainly as the process is going on but even in the immediate but electorally untested aftermath of the adoption of a new map.

Any reform proposal in any area of interest depends on the normative views of the reformer. We favor competitive elections in which each party nominates a qualified candidate who can make his or her views and qualifications known to the electorate. The redistricting processes currently used in most of the states fail to meet that standard. They are dominated either by political parties or by incumbents; neither favors more competition. Parties want to reduce the number of seats in which they must wage expensive campaigns. Incumbents do not want to lose. Both goals argue for establishing the largest number of safe seats.[28]

We believe that a redistricting process that takes power away from those who have a clear incentive to restrict competition would have a most beneficial impact on the electoral process. From our perspective, the appropriate mechanism would be to encourage more highly qualified candidates to think seriously about running for the House—or at the very least, not to discourage them from running. Were such a process in place in more states, fewer candidates would be discouraged by the partisan makeup of the district; fewer would be discouraged by concern for the impact of redistricting. We fully understand that a reform of this type would have a minimal effect (at least for congressional elections) in many states. We also are not so naïve as to overlook the political difficulty of reforming the redistricting process in this manner in many states.

However, there are relatively few institutional changes that can truly affect competition in U.S. elections. The quality of our democracy is called into question when 99 percent of the incumbents seeking reelection gain reelection—15 to 20 percent of them without any competition whatsoever—and only 10 percent of them run in competitive races. If Americans truly believe in the democratic principles they profess, they must take on the battles necessary to make congressional elections more competitive and responsive to changes in the views of the electorate.

Notes

1. Robert A. Dahl, *Polyarchy: Participation and Opposition* (Yale University Press, 1971).

2. Alan I. Abramowitz and Brad Alexander, "Incumbency, Redistricting, and the Decline of Competition in Congressional Elections: Evidence from the 2002 Midterm Election," paper presented at the 2004 Annual Meeting of the Western Political Science Association, Portland, Oregon, March 11–13, 2004.

3. 2005 Spring Goldfarb Lecture, Colby College, Waterville, Maine, April 18, 2005 (www.colby.edu/goldfarbcenter). See also "2006 Competitive House Race Chart," *Cook Political Report*, March 11, 2005 (www.cookpolitical.com/races/report_pdfs/2006_house_summary_chart_march11.pdf).

4. *CQ Politics Today* (now *CQ Politics Weekly*), April 2, 2004, an electronic newsletter distributed by Congressional Quarterly Service.

5. The 2004 Texas gerrymander is a classic example of the "stacking and cracking" method of gerrymandering, identified by Bruce E. Cain, *The Reapportionment Puzzle* (University of California Press, 1984), albeit with a racial twist in this case.

6. Edward R. Tufte, "The Relationship between Seats and Votes in Two-Party Systems," *American Political Science Review* 67 (1973): 540; he was commenting on the effect noted in David Mayhew's seminal 1974 article, "Congressional Elections: The Case of the Vanishing Marginals," *Polity* 6 (1974): 295.

7. Paul S. Herrnson, *Party Campaigning in the 1980s* (Harvard University Press, 1988); Thomas A. Kazee and Mary C. Thornberry, "Where's the Party? Congressional Candidate Recruitment and American Party Organizations," *Western Political Quarterly* 43 (1990): 61–80; L. Sandy Maisel, "American Political Parties: Still Central to a Functioning Democracy?" in *American Political Parties: Decline or Resurgence?* edited by Jeffrey Cohen, Richard Fleisher, and Paul Cantor (Washington: CQ Press, 2001); L. Sandy Maisel, Cherie Maestas, and Walter J. Stone, "The Party Role in Congressional Competition," in *The Parties Respond: Changes in American Parties and Campaigns*, edited by L. Sandy Maisel (Boulder, Colo.: Westview Press, 2002); Walter J. Stone and others, "Prospects, Money, Candidate Entry, and Vote Share in U.S. House Elections: What's Causing What?" paper presented at the 2004 Annual Meeting of the Western Political Science Association, Portland, Oregon, March 11–13, 2004.

8. L. Sandy Maisel, *From Obscurity to Oblivion: Running in the Congressional Primary*, 2nd ed. (University of Tennessee Press, 1986); Linda L. Fowler and Robert McClure, *Political Ambition: Who Decides to Run for Congress* (Yale University Press, 1989); Linda L. Fowler, *Candidates, Congress, and the American Democracy* (University of Michigan Press, 1993).

9. In the 202 districts in which an incumbent was seeking reelection in 2004 and for which the filing deadline had passed as of March 31, the total number of candidates who filed to run in the major party challenging the incumbent was 209. In twenty-seven of those districts, no one filed as a major party opponent of the incumbent; in the other 175 districts, the average number of candidates seeking the nomination to oppose an incumbent was under 1.2.

10. The cost of running can be measured in many ways—time, money, lost opportunity, political capital, and so forth.

11. "2004 House Overview," *Cook Political Report*, February 24, 2004, p. 1.

12. L. Sandy Maisel and Walter J. Stone, "The Politics of Government-Funded Research: Notes from the Experience of the Candidate Emergence Study," *PS: Political Science and Politics*, December 1998 (www.apsanet.org/PS/dec98/maiselstone.cfm).

13. The methodology used in identifying candidates for the current study mirrors that which we used successfully in our study of potential candidates in the 1998 election; a subset of the respondents in our current data set was drawn from the first study, which represented a pioneering means of identifying potential candidates for office, whether they eventually chose to run or not. In the summer of 1997, we conducted two surveys, designed to examine the decisionmaking of potential candidates for the 1998 congressional elections. The first, the Informant Survey, was sent to a sample of political activists in a random sample of 200 congressional districts. Our goal was to find ten Democratic and ten Republican activists in each district, individuals who were likely to be knowledgeable about congressional races but not likely to run themselves. We drew our sample from 1996 convention delegates and a listing of county chairs. We originally also added to our sample political journalists and political scientists living in the district who studied American politics. After our pretest we eliminated the journalists from the sample because a number of those polled raised ethical concerns about their participation. We eliminated the political scientists because a high percentage of our colleagues pleaded ignorance of real world decisionmaking in their home districts.

We asked the activists to give us information about the district and the incumbent and then to list up to four individuals who they felt would be strong candidates for the House of Representatives, whether those individuals had ever been mentioned as a candidate or not. We also asked a series of questions about why they thought that those individuals were strong potential candidates. Later we polled the 1,400 PCs named by our informants for whom we could locate usable addresses, repeating questions about the district and the incumbent and then asking a longer series of questions about the PCs themselves. We followed parallel procedures for the two surveys. All surveys were conducted by mail. The Informant Survey was sent early in the summer of 1997. The Potential Candidate Survey was mailed using a rolling sample; PCs were contacted within two to three months of the filing deadline in their states. In each case we sent an approach letter to the respondent explaining the purpose of the study, followed immediately by a questionnaire packet that included a self-addressed stamped envelope. One week after the survey packet was mailed, we sent reminder postcards. Within about a month after the first mailing, we sent a second packet to all of those who had not responded.

The Informant Survey had a response rate of 43 percent and yielded 1,399 unique potential candidates in 192 of our 200 sampled districts. The Potential Candidate Survey had a response rate of 32.3 percent, with 452 usable responses. We have explored potential response bias by comparing informant-generated data on PCs who did respond with data on those who did not respond, with reassuring results. See Walter J. Stone and L. Sandy Maisel, "The Not-So-Simple Calculus of Winning: Potential U.S. House Candidates' Nomination and General Election Chances," *Journal of Politics* 65 (November 2003): 951–77, for a more detailed discussion of the survey methodology used in the first round of surveys. In the Potential Candidate Survey, we asked questions about the partisan composition of the district as one of the factors that might encourage or deter a PC thinking about a race for the House.

In 1999 we went back into the field, seeking to reassess our findings and asking questions about the impact of changes in context that had occurred in the ensuing two years, including but not limited to changes in the level of trust in and prestige of government institutions as a result of the Clinton impeachment imbroglio. For this 2000 wave of the Candidate Emergence Study, we returned to the districts from which we had gotten responses to the previous wave.

Finally in 2001, we returned to the field once more, again building on our panel but also increasing the size of our sample by oversampling in districts deemed likely to be competitive. Of course, because we were in the field in the summer sixteen months before the 2002 election, we had only rough estimates of which districts were likely to be competitive come election day. We relied on best guesses from Stuart Rothenberg of the *Rothenberg Political Report*, Amy Walter of the *Cook Political Report*, and Rhodes Cook of the *Rhodes Cook Newsletter* in selecting our districts. In this third round, we surveyed in 154 congressional districts. For this analysis we rely totally on this third set of surveys.

14. For the 2002 Potential Candidate Survey, our overall response rate was 33.5 percent (1,537 of 4,532). The PCs came from various sources—state legislators representing constituencies within our sample districts (29 percent response rate); those identified by the respondents that we surveyed (40 percent response rate); PC respondents to our previous surveys, that is, our PC panel (55 percent response rate); respondents who identified themselves as potential candidates (58 percent response rate); and those identified through Web sources as likely to run (51 percent response rate).

As in our 1998 and 2000 surveys, a majority of those we surveyed (59.3 percent) and a majority of our respondents (53.4 percent) were state legislators, included in the list of PCs because more candidates for Congress come from the state legislatures than from any other single source. But most state legislators do not run, and most candidates come from other sources. Nearly 20 percent of our PC respondents were individuals identified from our 2002 Informant Survey, a percentage that would be increased if we added those in our panel originally identified in this manner. Two-thirds of those PCs would not have been picked up from any other source, a testament to the success of the method we use to identify strong potential candidates who do not enter the process through other easily recognized paths.

15. We also are interested in how district conditions and changes affect ambitions for office, but that is beyond the scope of our analysis in this chapter.

16. For a fuller discussion of redistricting processes, see Michael McDonald," A Comparative Analysis of Redistricting Institutions in the United States, 2001–02," *State Politics and Policy Quarterly* 4 (2004): 4.

17. States with redistricting commissions include Arizona, Connecticut, Hawaii, Idaho, Indiana, Iowa, Maryland, Minnesota, New Jersey, Rhode Island, and Washington. States with redistricting settled by the courts include Colorado, Mississippi, Texas, Wisconsin, South Carolina, and New Mexico. Information on redistricting process was drawn from the National Council of State Legislatures redistricting website (www.ncsl.org/programs/legman/elect/statesites.htm).

18. Of course, it is possible that the partisan bias apparent in table 2-1 is driving some of the results in table 2-2. The table below, however, presents an ordinary least squares model of the change in boundaries that controls for the partisanship of the respondent as well as the type of redistricting process in the state. The dependent variable is the full seven-point response scale form asking respondents about the effect of redistricting on candidates in their district. The scale ranges from *strongly favor Democrats* (–3) to *strongly favor Republicans* (+3). Party identification is scored on a five-point scale with higher values indicating a stronger identification with the Republican Party. The redistricting context is captured by several variables in the model: whether the redistricting process is controlled by the legislature; the party of the legislature; and an interaction between legislative party and legislative redistricting. If partisan redistricting processes are conditioning the perceptions of potential candidates, we should find the interaction effect significant and the main effects insignificant. In other words, it is the condition of legislative redistricting combined with the party of the legislature that produces the expectation. Clearly, the table below shows such an effect.

PC Perception That Redistricting Favors Republican Candidates

Variable	b (SE)	Significance
Party identification of PC	.138 (.03)	***
Party control of legislature (Democrat = −1, split = 0; Republican = +1)	.180 (.14)	
Legislature controls redistricting process	.071 (.163)	
Party control 3 legislative control	.445 (.158)	**
Court-controlled redistricting	.193 (.211)	
Constant	−.209 (.167)	
Number of cases	728	
F statistic	21.28	***
Adjusted R^2	.1224	

**$p < .01$; *** $p < .001$.

19. We note that if those drawing the boundaries are following the most common theories regarding partisan gerrymandering, those who see Democrats as gaining even though Republicans control the process may well have the same expectations as those drawing the lines. One strategy clearly is to pack the districts of some incumbents in the other party with their partisan followers in order to leave fewer of that party for the other districts.

20. We have coded the item extremes .01 (*extremely unlikely*) and .99 (*extremely likely*), and the midpoint .50 (*toss up*). The two categories on either side of .50 are equidistant between the extreme and the midpoint. The coding we have adopted is inevitably a rough approximation of the underlying subjective probabilities that we are attempting to measure. It has the virtue of producing data that are readily interpretable and consistent with the verbal cues that we gave respondents in wording the questions.

However, caution must be exercised when interpreting the results. In order to distinguish between the theoretical probabilities of interest and these subjective "pseudo-probabilities," we refer to them as "electoral prospects" or "chances." They are not estimates of the probabilities of the events described in our questions, but they can capture relative differences in the subjective prospects of incumbents and potential candidates.

21. Gary C. Jacobson and Samuel Kernell, *Strategy and Choice in Congressional Election* (Yale University Press, 1983); Gary C. Jacobson, "The Marginals Never Vanished: Incumbency and Competition in Elections to the U.S. House of Representatives, 1952–1982," *American Journal of Political Science* 31 (1987): 126–41.

22. This is similar to the finding we demonstrate in Stone and Maisel, "The Not-So-Simple Calculus of Winning."

23. We asked potential candidates to assess the partisan balance of their district prior to the 2002 redistricting on a five-point scale. Districts that lean clearly toward one of the parties are coded as 1 while those remaining are coded as 0.

24. Table 2-7 was derived from these responses: of the 1,128 valid responses, 576 respondents expected redistricting to favor his or her party; of those, 476 were "certain" or "pretty certain" about their district boundaries while 118 were still "uncertain." A total of 286 respondents expected redistricting to favor neither party; 221 were at least "pretty certain" about district changes while 65 were "uncertain." Finally, 266 respondents expected redistricting to favor the opposition party; 229 were at least "pretty certain" about district changes while 37 were "uncertain."

25. States with smaller populations tend to be politically homogeneous in any case. Of the twelve states with either one or two representatives, eight (if one includes the somewhat idiosyncratic Vermont) have congressional delegations all from one party; two of these states have split Senate delegations, and the other two have senators from one party and House member(s) from the other—as in the somewhat odd case of Maine, which has two Republican senators and two Democratic representatives.

26. It should be noted, however, that changes in the redistricting procedure could well be reflected in changes in the procedure used for redistricting state legislatures as well, in which case they would be as important for these states as any others.

27. See Stone and Maisel, "The Not-So-Simple Calculus of Winning."

28. This argument holds for those states in which a court or some other body intervenes if the partisan bodies are unable to reach agreement, presumably because of partisan balance among those making the decisions. The reversion to a nonpartisan decisionmaker is a matter of the political circumstance of the moment, not of a commitment to competitive elections as a goal.

Pushbutton Gerrymanders? How Computing Has Changed Redistricting

Micah Altman, Karin Mac Donald, and Michael McDonald

Following the 2001 round of redistricting, observers across the political spectrum warned that computing technology had fundamentally changed redistricting, for the worse. Their concern was that computers have enabled the crafting of finely drawn redistricting plans that promote partisan and career goals to the detriment of electoral competition, ultimately thwarting voters' ability to express their will through the ballot box.

For decades, the Supreme Court has considered the issue of computers in redistricting. In 1969, Justice Harlan wrote, "A computer may grind out district lines which can totally frustrate the popular will on an overwhelming number of critical issues."[1] In the Court's recent redistricting decision, *Vieth* v. *Jubelirer*, Justice Breyer amplified that claim: "The availability of enhanced computer technology allows the parties to redraw boundaries in ways that target individual neighborhoods and homes, carving out safe but slim victory margins in the maximum number of districts, with little risk of cutting their margins too thin."[2] Some observers of redistricting have concluded

We thank Burt Monroe, Bruce Cain, and Thomas Mann for their helpful comments and Nicole Boyle and Tamina Alon for their excellent research assistance.

that "[g]errymandering is not self-regulating anymore . . . the software has become too good."[3]

Although the claims about the corrupting power of computers in redistricting are often repeated, no one has rigorously examined the evidence. Have computers really changed redistricting? Is this now a world of push-button gerrymanders? Are gerrymanders more effective, more aesthetically appealing, and more durable because of computer technology?

In previous work, we reported the results of a survey that we conducted to establish the facts of computer use in redistricting.[4] We researched state redistricting authorities in 1991 and 2001 and described the key patterns of computer use and the fundamental capabilities of computer redistricting systems. Our investigation shows that use of computers was practically universal in the 1991 round of redistricting. By the 2001 round, mapping software had become substantially faster and cheaper, but its fundamental capabilities had not changed dramatically. The timing of the almost universal adoption of computers and the relative continuity of computer capabilities suggest that much of the blame assigned to computers for modern redistricting excesses has been misplaced.

The possibility remains that computer use, along with maps drawn using election data, has significant and complex effects on redistricting outcomes. While technological innovations and benefits allowed redistricters to create maps at greatly diminished time and expense, from a quantitative standpoint it is difficult to directly assess the impact of those innovations on redistricting because of the nearly universal adoption of geographical information systems (GIS) during the 1991 redistricting cycle. Instead, we use the variation in the availability of electoral data and in the capabilities of the computer systems used to tease out the effects of computing on district compactness and competitiveness.

In this chapter, we present a brief historical overview of computer use in redistricting and the fundamental capabilities of computer systems. We then use our previous survey data, along with data on the compactness and competitiveness of congressional redistricting plans, to determine the effects that computer use has had on traditional redistricting criteria.[5]

A Brief History of Computers in Redistricting

Between 1980 and 2000, computer systems went from being rare and expensive "toys," useful only for demonstration purposes, to being cheap, powerful, ubiquitous, standardized, off-the-shelf systems available to nearly everyone. Computers were first used in redistricting in the 1960s, although their use did not become widespread until the 1991 round of redistricting. Political scientists in the early 1960s first advocated the use of computers as an *antidote* to gerrymandering.[6] Software capable of performing automated redistricting was deployed, in a limited fashion, by at least three state legislatures in 1971. However, automation proved an elusive goal, and those systems were generally used simply for data tabulation. By 1981, only a handful of states used redistricting computer systems.

Computer use expanded in 1991 when all but four states—Idaho, New Hampshire, New Jersey, and Vermont—adopted computers for congressional or state legislative redistricting. System customizations and capabilities varied tremendously; some software packages did little more than display maps on the screen, while others provided detailed, interactive demographic and geographic reports. Some states used their state planning departments' software, but those systems were not specialized for the task of redistricting and required modification to calculate newly imposed redistricting criteria, such as compactness. Other states hired consulting firms to develop specialized redistricting applications.

Despite the widespread use of computers in 1991, access to them was quite limited. Redistricting computing was expensive; it required high-end computers and ongoing programming assistance and technical support. Few states provided public terminals for the public to participate in the process, and few outside groups could afford to purchase their own systems.

By 2001, a GIS software revolution allowed more companies to compete in the niche market for redistricting software. Prices dropped sharply, and redistricting mapping applications became over-the-counter merchandise that could run on any semi-current home computer. Personal computers had dropped dramatically in price and had become tremendously more powerful. The same computing power delivered by a mainframe computer in 1991 could be delivered by a mid-range laptop in 2001, for a fraction of the price. Any interested organization could now afford computer hardware and redistricting software.

Lower costs enabled greater dissemination of the technology. All states except Michigan reported using redistricting software in 2000. Michigan's response to our survey indicated that the state did not purchase redistricting software because its affordability allowed private organizations and political parties to buy their own. By 2001, through on-screen click-and-point applications, mapping software also had become easier to use. Within a few hours, a computer novice could acquire enough skill to draw a redistricting plan. The drop in the price of hardware and software combined with the ease of use of new redistricting applications, and the availability of state websites for disseminating data, maps, and meeting schedules opened participation in the redistricting process to a wider array of political actors and the general public.

Software Capabilities

While faster and easier to use, the computer systems employed in the most recent round of redistricting did not offer radically new functionality. Redistricting software developed through 1981 was used primarily for tabulation by district of data such as race or population data. Advances in GIS in the mid-1980s enabled in 1991 thematic mapping, on-screen color-coding of geography by data that would previously have been simply tabulated. Almost every 2001 redistricting package offered a relatively standard set of core capabilities in five broad functional categories: tabulation of district population and registration; thematic mapping; geographic reporting and error checking; and automated generation of plans.

Tabulation and thematic mapping are basic capabilities now found in all redistricting software, as are geographic reports that calculate measures of compactness or detect errors, such as noncontiguous or unassigned geography. Table 3-1 reports that in the 2000 round of redistricting, approximately 90 percent of states used software with those capabilities. Almost half of the states used software with automated redistricting capability, which has been the subject of commentary by pundits. A typical warning:

> Mappers were able to specify a desired outcome or outcomes—the number of people in a district, say, or the percentage of Democrats in it—and have the program design a potential new district instantly. These systems allow redistricters to create hundreds of rough drafts easily and quickly, and to choose from among them maps that are both politically and aesthetically appealing.[7]

Our assessment is that the capabilities of automated redistricting are greatly exaggerated.[8] A fundamental technical difficulty is the lack of efficient and effective automated redistricting algorithms. The most straightforward technique generates some or all of the possible districts by using a partition-generating function. Those that do not meet legal criteria, such as those

Table 3-1. *Capabilities of Computer Systems Used in 2000 Congressional and Legislative Redistricting*
Percent

Type of redistricting	Thematic mapping	Geographic reports and data tabulation	Automated redistricting
Congressional	100	88.1	47.62
Number of cases	42	37	20
Legislative	100	90	50
Number of cases	50	45	23

Source: Authors' survey, on file. See chapter note 5.

containing noncontiguous districts, are eliminated. However, the underlying mathematical problem is extremely complex. Because of that, any automated redistricting algorithm is guaranteed to find the best solution only for extremely limited problems.[9]

Simplifying the redistricting problem sidesteps mathematical complexity. However, simplification is not easy in the United States, where the legal demand for population equality is quite stringent and redistricting plans often must simultaneously satisfy several conflicting federal criteria, such as equal population and compliance with the Voting Rights Act (VRA), and state constitutional criteria, such as compactness, respect for city and county boundaries, and respect for communities of interest. No automated redistricting software commercially available in 2001 was capable of optimizing more than one criterion—and our testing experience indicated that they did so poorly—making such software irrelevant for practical consideration. Only one custom program, developed by the Texas Legislative Council, was capable of multicriteria redistricting, and the program functioned poorly in generating a map for the entire state. Even if fully functional automated software were available, we suspect that none of those currently in charge of redistricting would relinquish their authority to a computer, given the high political stakes involved.

Redistricting Data

Redistricting is a data-intensive task. To create a viable redistricting plan, volumes of data are analyzed to determine whether a plan meets a variety of legal criteria, such as equal population, VRA, and state requirements.

Computers were first used to tabulate census population data, and tabulation of data remains a core feature of redistricting software.

Computers and redistricting were brought together at a fortuitous point in American political development. Just as the U.S. Supreme Court articulated an equal population standard for districts in a series of court cases in the 1960s, computing technology crawled out of its infancy to aid in tabulating the data. The basis for determining equal population is, of course, the decennial census of the U.S. population, and the release of new census data at the beginning of a decade now triggers redistricting activity at all levels of government. Race and ethnicity data also are used, to satisfy provisions of the Voting Rights Act. The PL94-171 file, named after the public law mandating its release, provides total population and population by voting age, race, and ethnicity at the census block level, which is roughly equivalent to a city block in urban areas but larger in rural areas. Along with population data, the Bureau of the Census provides maps of census geography, which since 1990 have been released in an electronic format known as the TIGER (topographically integrated geographic encoding and referencing) file. These geographical units literally become the building blocks of districts.

The PL94-171 population data do not contain political data or any other data that might describe the population in more detail, such as educational attainment or socioeconomic status. Census demographic data are released later, after redistricting is complete in most states. Most redistricting entities, whether a political party, a state legislature, or a redistricting commission, "enhance" population data by merging it with political data such as election or voter registration information, which is reported by precinct. However, those data are not easily merged, since census blocks do not necessarily correspond to electoral or registration precincts. Some but not all states participate in a census program to define voting precincts in terms of census geography; the resulting units are known as voting tabulation districts (VTDs). The correspondence between election precincts and VTDs (and consequently blocks) usually is reliable only for the most recent elections. Furthermore, voting and registration precincts may not have identical boundaries. In those cases, heuristics and statistical algorithms can be employed to match census and election data. Creating such custom data sets is expensive, time consuming, and computer intensive, but it may be necessary to forecast the political consequences of a redistricting plan and to assess its compliance with the Voting Rights Act.

Other official redistricting criteria, which vary by state constitution or statute, are compactness, contiguity, respect for communities of interest, preservation of city and county boundaries, and alignment with geographic features. Once districts have been defined in terms of census geography, the geospatial data contained in the TIGER files can be manipulated to confirm that districts are contiguous and to create measures of compactness. City, county, and most geographic features are defined in the TIGER files. The communities-of-interest criterion is neither well defined nor easy to apply. Among practitioners and scholars, there is no common definition of this redistricting principle, and implementation is severely constrained by lack of data.

Measuring the Effect of Computing on Congressional Redistricting

Our investigation of the effect of computers on redistricting is constrained by practical considerations. First, our analysis is limited to the rounds of redistricting covered by our survey: those that took place in 1991 and 2001. Second, it includes only congressional district data. The limited scope of our analysis therefore prevents us from directly testing the effect of computers on congressional redistricting. All states that conducted congressional redistricting in 1991—with the exception of Idaho, New Hampshire, and New Jersey—used a computer system, and all used computers in 2001. Without variation, we cannot test for an effect, since in essence there is nothing to be explained.

Although computer use itself was ubiquitous by 2001, there were variations in its use: whether a state developed an in-house computer system, the capabilities of the particular computer system involved (which is known for 2001, but not for 1991), and whether the state used an election database in conjunction with its redistricting effort. Table 3-2 shows the overall pattern of variation in redistricters' data use by summarizing their responses to our survey. From 1991 to 2001, all indicators of redistricting sophistication increased. We used this variation in computer use to tease out the effects of computers on redistricting plans themselves. In particular, we modeled the effects of computer use on the compactness and competitiveness of redistricting plans.

Competitiveness

A recent concern is that computing technology permits such fine slicing and dicing of a state's political geography that election outcomes are essentially predetermined. The editorial pages of the *New York Times* issued a typical warning: "Using powerful computers, line-drawers can now determine,

Table 3-2. *Summary of Survey Results Regarding Redistricters' Use of Data and Consultants*[a]

Percent

Type of redistricting	Manual redis- tricting	Used voting data	Used registration data	Used other data	Used consultants to perform redistricting	Used block data
1992 Congressional	5.3	71.4	64.3	21	31.6	66.7
Number of cases	2	30	27	8	12	23
1992 Legislative	9.3	64.6	58.3	20.9	31.1	46.2
Number of cases	4	31	28	9	14	24
2002 Congressional	0	72.7	75	26.2	13.2	71
Number of cases	0	32	33	11	5	27
2002 Legislative	0	66	68	24	15.2	53.9
Number of cases	0	33	34	12	7	28

Source: Authors' survey, on file. See chapter note 5.
a. Numbers of cases are absolute counts.

with nearly scientific precision, how many loyal party voters need to be stuffed into any given district to make it impregnable."[10]

Several measures have been used to evaluate the competitiveness of electoral systems and districts: the number of competitive elections, the bias and responsiveness of the estimated seats-votes curve, and the number of competitive districts. The argument that computerized redistricting has resulted in fewer competitive elections does not jibe well with the timing of the influx of computing technology, by several measures. Responsiveness and bias were clearly displaying a worsening trend by the 1980s, before any substantial use of computers.[11] Sophisticated computer operations were used in nearly every state in 1991, yet the number of competitive House contests increased. In the 2000 round of redistricting, computer use was qualitatively very similar to that in the 1990s round, but the number of competitive House contests dropped substantially.[12] However, the widespread adoption of computers in the 1990s does correspond to a disturbing decrease in the number of competitive *districts*, which is one determining factor in the competitiveness of elections and a factor that redistricters have considerable control over.

Given the timing of its adoption, computing technology seems unlikely to be the primary culprit for changes in competitiveness. Still, technology could be a contributing factor. In this chapter we evaluate the conventional wisdom that redistricting has reduced the number of competitive districts by measuring district competitiveness and comparing it with aspects of computer use. Measuring the political leaning of districts from election data is a relatively straightforward task, and such measures often are used to forecast the political effects of a redistricting map. We used a standard measure, the percentage of the 2002 congressional districts in a state within a 45 to 55 percent range of the "normalized presidential vote," which is the Democratic share of the Democratic plus Republican vote adjusted to the national mean for the 2000 presidential election. (For further discussion of the measure, see chapter 1 of this volume.)

Conventional wisdom implies that if computers enable those drawing district lines to fine-tune district lines to reduce competitiveness, certain aspects of computer use are associated with fewer competitive districts. Conventional wisdom also suggests that states that developed redistricting software, particularly in 1991, exhibit high sophistication and a possible intent to gerrymander. Because election data would be a valuable tool in trying to affect a political outcome, one might expect the creation of such a database to be associated with fewer competitive districts. Tabulation capabilities would provide the necessary statistics to assess political effects. To fine-tune a map, one might expect that district lines would be precisely drawn down to the census block level in order to realize every last ounce of electoral gain. As before, we would expect little use of automated redistricting algorithms and thus no correlation with competition.

Compactness

A common complaint about redistricting is that it produces bizarrely shaped districts. The crab-shaped 2002 Illinois 17th congressional district is emblematic of the issue. The district stretches hundreds of miles across the farmland of western Illinois and at one point cuts a block-wide swath through Springfield's shopping malls and golf courses, without picking up population, to capture areas of Decatur to the east. Districts that carefully divide voters expose the role of politics in redistricting. The U.S. Supreme Court, in addressing racial gerrymandering in *Miller* v. *Johnson*, placed special emphasis on "traditional redistricting principles" such as "compactness, contiguity, respect for political subdivisions or communities defined by actual shared interests" and considered violation of compactness an indicator of possibly unconstitutional racial gerrymandering.[13] However, violations of "traditional redistricting principles" are neither prohibited by the U.S. Constitution nor by federal law, although those principles may often be found in state constitutions and statutes.

Compactness is often claimed to help prevent—and lack thereof to indicate—political or racial gerrymandering. Since many gerrymanders are easily identified by their unique shapes, which are anything but "box-like," it was assumed that holding redistricters to compact shapes would minimize "voter-picking'" along political or racial lines. As a consequence, statisticians and political scientists embarked on an effort to define "compactness."

One difficulty in implementing a compactness standard is that there are multiple ways of measuring compactness.[14] We developed two compactness measures by manipulating the TIGER files describing the 103rd and 108th congressional districts.[15] One measure calculates the ratio of the normalized area to the perimeter of the district, which we refer to as PA.[16] The other is the ratio of the district area to the area of the minimum circumscribing circle, which we call by the name of its inventor, Reock.[17] Both measures lie on a [0,1] interval, with a higher value associated with a higher degree of compactness. These measures capture different aspects of a district's shape, but they are strongly and significantly correlated at the district level. The unit of our analysis is the state, and we averaged the compactness measures across all districts within a state. Both measures are strongly correlated at the state level, and both are weakly but significantly correlated with competitiveness.[18]

Although we are interested in the role that computers play in measuring compactness, little existing research explained variation in compactness among states. Niemi and others investigated the measurement of compactness across states,[19] and Altman demonstrated how compactness scores varied over the course of U.S. history.[20] A compactness standard has been used as an independent variable in other analyses of redistricting output.[21] Our analysis more broadly probes the factors that influence the creation of compact districts.

Conventional wisdom might suggest that more sophisticated in-house computer operations would be capable of fine-tuning their lines politically, producing less compact districts. Similarly, we expected that states that use political data and population data on the block level (rather than the tract or VTD level, for example) would be more likely to be tuned to a political purpose and capable of finely slicing and dicing a state, which would result in less compact districts.

We evaluate our expectations with an important caveat. As we pointed out in our previous research, much of the dramatic change in district appearance over the last thirty years preceded the use of computers.[22] The trend toward decreasing compactness started in the mid-1960s, with the introduction of the equal population and majority-minority district requirements.[23] The adoption of computing technology, however, is coterminous with the increase in districts with questionable contiguity—those connected by water or a single point.

Analysis

For the sake of exposition, we simplified our analysis to examine only two-way relationships between competitiveness or compactness measures and aspects of computer use. A more complete approach would use statistical tools to control for other potentially confounding effects, such as the type of gerrymander, Voting Rights Act concerns, the competitiveness or shape of the state, and many other factors. In an unpublished multivariate analysis, we found relationships similar to those reported in this chapter.

We used a difference of means test to determine whether competitiveness or compactness is greater or less in the presence and absence of an aspect of computer use (full results are presented in the appendix to this chapter). We generally found no difference in district competitiveness and compactness across computer use in the states. Contrary to conventional wisdom, competitiveness and compactness were better by small but statistically significant ($p < .05$) amounts when redistricters used census block data rather than larger geographic units. The distribution of compactness scores also suggests that plans were slightly more compact (and perhaps more competitive) when a computer system supported automated redistricting. (See the appendix for summary statistics and for plots showing the corresponding distributions of compactness and competitiveness scores.) However, this finding was statistically significant for only one of our two compactness measures, PA ($p = .10$, one-tailed).

What accounts for our findings? We speculate that when using larger units of analysis, redistricters are more constrained in their ability to produce box-like districts. Units that are larger than blocks, such as precincts, are less "pretty" in their geography and consequently end up building less pretty districts. This is especially true when entire counties are used to build districts. The irregular geographies of counties not only produce irregular shapes in districts, but their use also prevents redistricters from slicing off smaller pockets of desirable communities. Consequently, line drawers are also less likely to achieve a "perfect" political makeup in a district because larger units of analysis inevitably mean more people, with often larger variations in their political affiliations. Given a choice between drawing a district that is too competitive or one that is not competitive enough, redistricters err on the side of caution and draw districts that are less competitive. Similarly, a more compact district might be achieved by slicing a county in two, whereas adding an entire county may unnecessarily increase the perimeter of a district. Redistricters may also anticipate complaints about the compactness of the districts that they draw and therefore use the tools available to them to draw compact districts that still achieve their political goals.

Conclusion

Adapting an old National Rifle Association slogan, we might observe that "computers don't gerrymander, people do." A systematic analysis of the extent and effect of computer use in redistricting reveals that the courts' fears and pundits' claims are somewhat overblown. The use of computers did not change dramatically in the last round of redistricting—nor did the capabilities of redistricting systems. While there has been a dramatic decrease in the cost and increase in the speed of computing, there have been marginal changes only (with the exception of limited automated redistricting) in the range of features supported and in the power of the analyses provided by computers. The automated redistricting capabilities that some feared would produce instant, attractive gerrymanders have not yet materialized: current packages cannot produce even adequate redistricting plans satisfactorily, and they cannot compete with line drawing by human beings. However, the sophistication of the automated system in Texas may foreshadow a change in how optimal gerrymandering can be achieved.

Moreover, the timing of the adoption of computers in redistricting does not jibe with the timing of the major changes in district competitiveness and compactness that have occurred in recent decades. Indeed, if anything, we find that computers may be beneficial to redistricting. Block-level databases appear to provide mapdrawers more options for configuring geography, which in turn may have enabled the drawing of more competitive and more compact districts in 1991 and 2001. Other aspects of computer use are generally unrelated to the drawing of competitive or compact districts.

In this context, computers are only a tool, not an end in themselves. They may expand the set of possible redistricting plans, but that does not mean that those in charge have to choose any particular one. The real choices are made by those drawing the districts, who, we imagine, may be heard to say, borrowing from a past National Rifle Association president: "You can pry my computer from my cold, dead hands."

Appendix: Statistical Details

Figure 1 compares the mean levels of competitiveness and compactness (with accompanying standard errors) for states using or not using voting data, block data, and consultants. Figure 2 compares states using or not using GIS reports and automated redistricting. In each figure, column 1 compares levels of competitiveness while column 2 compares levels of compactness. (We show the PA measure of compactness in these figures. Similar findings for the Reock measure are not displayed, but the data are available in our replication data set; see endnote 5.) As a general rule, the relationship between competitiveness or compactness with an aspect of computer use is considered statistically significant if the difference between the two means is large compared with the standard errors of each mean.

These figures show ten graphs that summarize the distribution of compactness and competitive scores for states using different levels of technology and data. We summarize these distributions using Tukey box-plots.[24] Each graph comprises two side-by-side box plots, which compare the distribution of scores in states with more than three districts that use a selected technology to the distribution in those that do not use that technology. The middle line in each box plot shows the median score for states using or not using each technology. The "box" portion of the graph contains the central 50 percent of the distribution, and the width of the box is proportional to the number of states using or not using that technology. (Each plot also shows the individual datapoints, with a small amount of random horizontal "jitter" added for display purposes. The smaller lines show the mean and standard deviation.)

Figure 1. *Comparison of the Compactness and Competitiveness of 1991 and 2001 Congressional Districts by Use of Voting Data, Block Data, and Consultant*

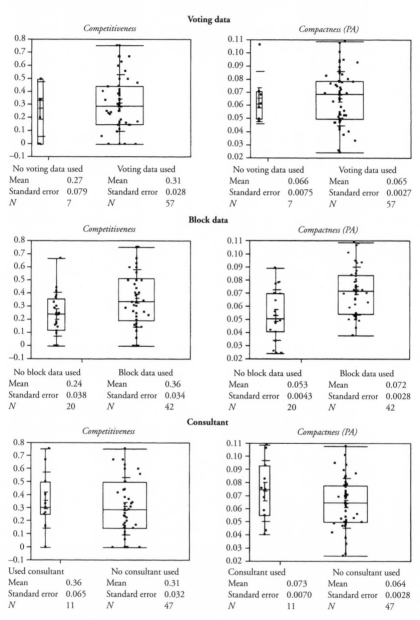

Figure 2. *Comparison of the Compactness and Competitiveness of 1991 and 2001 Congressional Districts by Use of GIS Reports and Automated Redistricting*

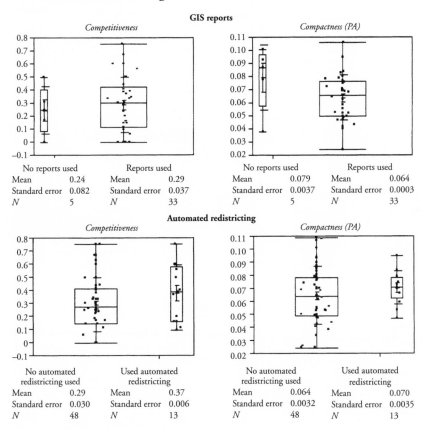

Notes

1. *Wells* v. *Rockefeller*, 349 U.S. 542 (1969).

2. *Vieth* v. *Jubelirer*, 541 U.S. 267 (2004).

3. Jeffrey Toobin, "The Great Election Grab," *New Yorker*, December 12, 2003, quoting Nathaniel Persily.

4. Micah Altman, Karin Mac Donald, and Michael P. McDonald, "Crayons to Computers: The Evolution of Computing in Redistricting," *Social Science Computer Review* 23, no. 2 (2005): 334–46.

5. Ibid. A replication data set with all information necessary to replicate the empirical results in this chapter, accompanied by a codebook containing the original survey instrument and coding details, will

be made available through the Inter-University Consortium for Political and Social Research (ICPSR), Publications Related Archive (www.icpsr.umich.edu/pra/> [July 5, 2005]).

6. William Vickrey, "On the Prevention of Gerrymandering," *Political Science Quarterly* 76 (March 1961): 105–11.

7. Don Peck and Casey Caitlin, "Packing, Cracking, and Kidnapping," *Atlantic Monthly*, January–February 2004.

8. Altman, Mac Donald, and McDonald, "Crayons to Computers."

9. See Micah Altman, "Is Automation the Answer? The Computational Complexity of Automated Redistricting," *Rutgers Computer and Law Technology Journal* 23, no.1 (1997): 81–142.

10. "Making Votes Count," *New York Times*, February 21, 2004, p. A14.

11. See, for example, Andrew Gelman and Gary King, "A Unified Method of Evaluating Electoral Systems and Redistricting Plans," *American Journal of Political Science* 38, no. 2 (1994): 540–41. Gelman and King show worsening trends (outside the South) beginning in the 1960s. The patterns of bias and responsiveness are cyclical and substantially improve after redistrictings, but they show an overall worsening trend over the decades.

12. Richard E. Cohen, "When Campaigns Are Cakewalks," *National Journal* 34, no. 11 (2002): 776–78.

13. *Miller v. Johnson*, 63 U.S.L.W. 4726 (1995).

14. Richard G. Niemi and others, "Measuring Compactness and the Role of a Compactness Standard in a Test for Partisan and Racial Gerrymandering," *Journal of Politics* 52, no. 4 (1990): 1155–81; H. P. Young, "Measuring the Compactness of Legislative Districts," *Legislative Studies Quarterly* 13, no. 1 (1988): 105–15.

15. U.S. Census cartographic boundary files were obtained from www.census.gov/geo/www/cob/. The compactness scores generated from those boundary files are included in our replication data.

16. Mark S. Flaherty and William W. Crumplin, "Compactness and Electoral Boundary Adjustment: An Assessment of Alternative Measures," *Canadian Geographer* 36, no. 2 (1992): 159–71.

17. Ernest C. Reock Jr., "A Note: Measuring Compactness as a Requirement of Legislative Reapportionment," *Midwest Journal of Political Science* 5, no. 1 (1961): 70–74.

18. The correlation between PA and REOCK is 0.73 ($p < .01$). The strong degree of correlation is expected for two measures of the same concept, compactness. The correlation between PA and percent competitive districts is 0.23 ($p = .07$) and between REOCK and percent competitive districts is 0.31 ($p = .01$).

19. Niemi and others, "Measuring Compactness and the Role of a Compactness Standard."

20. Micah Altman, "Traditional Districting Principles: Judicial Myths vs. Reality," *Social Science History* 22, no. 2 (1998): 159–200.

21. Jason Barabas and Jennifer Jerit, "Redistricting Principles and Racial Representation," *State Politics and Policy Quarterly* 4, no. 4 (2004): 415–36; Jamie L. Carson and Michael H. Crespin, "The Effect of State Redistricting Methods on Electoral Competition," *State Politics and Policy Quarterly* 4, no. 4 (2004): 455–70.

22. Altman, Mac Donald, and McDonald, "Crayons to Computers."

23. Altman, "Traditional Districting Principles."

24. J. W. Tukey, *Exploratory Data Analysis* (Reading, Mass.: Addison-Wesley, 1977).

Forty Years in the Political Thicket: Judicial Review of the Redistricting Process since *Reynolds* v. *Sims*

NATHANIEL PERSILY

Four decades after the Supreme Court established the one-person, one-vote rule, it seems fitting to evaluate the entire enterprise of judicial involvement in redistricting. This chapter attempts to identify consistent themes or tensions in the case law in order to bring to the surface subterranean pressures in the jurisprudence that find periodic expression in Supreme Court opinions. Taking a step back from the doctrinal debates, this chapter arrays the many redistricting decisions over the past forty years along three principal dimensions: rules versus standards, activism versus restraint, and individual rights versus group rights. These familiar conceptualizations of constitutional law complicate efforts to attach archetypal liberal-conservative labels to redistricting decisions. The chapter then provides a brief discussion of the relatively agreed-upon consequences of the courts' involvement in each subfield of redistricting litigation. After countless social scientific studies of the judicial role in redistricting, the impact of the courts' decisions can be assessed according to their effect on representation of certain groups (opposition parties, urban and suburban voters, racial minorities), their effect on intradistrict competition and competition for control of state legislatures, and their effect on the racialization of partisan conflicts.

Several caveats are in order at the outset. First, it is difficult to place sole blame or grant sole credit to the judiciary, as an institution, for any of the consequences of redistricting law. Congress, the executive branch, and state governments all play important roles in implementing court decisions, by setting the ground rules for judicial intervention—as with the Voting Rights Act (VRA)—or reacting to court decisions with new methods of achieving political goals that remain constant in the face of doctrinal change. Because its task is primarily to discuss the case law, this chapter focuses on the judiciary, but that focus should not detract from the obvious and overarching significance of political actors to the redistricting process. Second, this chapter may make the same mistake made in many others written on this topic: namely, inappropriately grouping a wide array of cases under the heading of redistricting and thereby obscuring the important differences between litigation under the Voting Rights Act, different provisions of the U.S. Constitution, and state laws. Although some of the conclusions herein can be generalized across redistricting law, others may be more properly compartmentalized within the constitutional or statutory provision at issue. Finally, by attempting to fit the case law into neat matrices or conceptual boxes, this chapter may go too far in trying to draw bright lines where what really exists are shades of gray. Redistricting law has gotten only more confusing and internally inconsistent in each of the census cycles since *Reynolds* v. *Sims*. By attempting to generalize about the case law in this area, this chapter necessarily glosses over some important complexities.

The Multiple Dimensions of Redistricting Case Law

The number of ways to analyze the redistricting case law is limited only by the number and ingenuity of law professors hoping to gain tenure by publishing studies on the topic. On their own, the redistricting cases have almost come to occupy a subdiscipline in U.S. law. By paying attention to three dimensions of the relevant case law, this chapter does not pretend to exhaust all the possible ways that the cases can be sliced and diced. Other arrays might include a liberal-conservative dimension, a textualist-interpretivist dimension, a representation-competition dimension, or even a race-party dimension. However, arraying the case law along the dimensions chosen here—rules-standards, activism-restraint, individual rights-group rights—

may help portray and explain the divisions on the current Supreme Court and situate the current state of the law along jurisprudential continua on which the Court has shifted ever since it first ventured into this particular political thicket.

Rules versus Standards

In the redistricting arena as in other areas of law, different judges (and therefore different precedents) will gravitate toward hard rules, at one end of the spectrum, or mushy standards, at the other.[1] Whereas those who favor rules might prefer a rigid trimester framework for abortion law, for example, standard-lovers might prefer an "undue burden" standard. Whereas some might prefer a rule of strict liability for certain accidents, others may gravitate toward a standard of negligence, founded on questions of what a reasonable person might be expected to do in such a circumstance. Indeed, the text of the Constitution itself provides a variety of standards: "republican form of government," "unreasonable searches and seizures," "due process," "excessive bail," and "cruel and unusual punishment." It also sometimes provides clear rules: age qualifications for office; the requirement that each state have exactly two senators; the requirement of a two-thirds vote of Congress to overturn a presidential veto; the provision that all criminal trials be done by jury; and the Thirteenth Amendment's ban on slavery.

So too with redistricting law. A threshold fight in the development of the case law is whether to adopt a rule or employ a flexible standard. Should the Court adopt a requirement of perfect population equality ("as equal as practicable" using the "best census data available") among districts or a seemingly more flexible standard, such as "substantial equality," to review claims of malapportionment? Should claims under section 2 of the VRA be limited by a rule that the minority community must constitute a numerical majority in a single-member district, or should a more flexible standard that focuses on "minority influence" constrain the redistricting process? Should retrogression under section 5 depend on a mechanical application of a rule that prohibits a decrease in the number of majority-minority districts or on a more flexible standard that gives states greater latitude in preventing a decrease in minority influence, broadly defined? And should partisan gerrymanders be held unconstitutional if they violate some rule of majoritarianism or proportional representation or only if they cannot surmount a flexible standard such as "consistently degrades a . . . group of voters' influence on the political process as a whole"?[2]

There are advantages and disadvantages to both approaches, of course. Rules usually provide for greater predictability, may be cheaper and more efficient to apply, and allow less discretion or bias to creep into the decisionmaking process. However, rules also run the risk of producing irrational results because of insensitivity to unique applications or inability to adapt to the facts of a particular case. Rulemaking may also be difficult in some areas of redistricting law where crystalline ex ante prescriptions may be impossible to formulate because of the unforeseen strategies that political actors devise to get around the rule.

Standards allow for greater attention to the facts of a given case and greater flexibility for the decisionmaker. As a result, they may lead to less uniformity in the case law, greater potential for bias, and less predictable results. However, the articulation of a standard may sometimes precede the codification of a rule. In other words, sometimes the Court may dip its toe into the shallow end with a standard before diving head first into the deep end with a rule. The Court's decisions in the one-person, one-vote cases and the constitutional race-based vote dilution cases described below may illustrate that approach. In the one-person, one-vote cases, the Court moved from an earlier standard of population equality to (seemingly) more rigid rules that forbid any unjustifiable deviations. In the constitutional racial vote dilution cases that preceded the 1983 amendments to the Voting Rights Act (*Whitcomb* v. *Chavis, White* v. *Regester,* and *Mobile* v. *Bolden*), the Court moved from a flexible, totality-of-the-circumstances standard to a rule that required a showing of discriminatory intent and effect.[3]

Of course, the rules-standards dimension represents a continuum, not a dichotomy. Many rules in the redistricting arena have some standard-like flexibility built into them. Even the one-person, one-vote rule itself, insofar as it allows for departures from perfect population equality for some legitimate state interests (for example, protection of political subdivision boundaries), suggests that it is somewhat more standard-like than its name suggests. That is all the more true in the context of noncongressional redistricting, as noted below. And insofar as demonstration of discriminatory effect allows for some kind of standard-like evaluation of influence on the political process, the rule preventing race-based vote dilution is not as mechanical as one might first expect.

Nevertheless, one can place redistricting precedents—and for that matter, the individual justices' opinions in these cases—along a rules-standards continuum. It is important to note at the outset, however, that the preference for rules over standards does not fall along predictable liberal-conservative lines, nor does a given justice's preference for rules or standards in one context of redistricting necessarily translate into the same preference in another context. Justice Sandra Day O'Connor, for example, whom many saw as the queen of judicial standards and case-by-case adjudication, would stick to a hard-and-fast rule of nonjusticiability in partisan gerrymandering cases. And Justice Antonin Scalia, who might be the king of rule-bound adjudication, would allow for the new, flexible standard of retrogression under section 5 of the VRA as detailed in *Georgia* v. *Ashcroft.*[4]

As the discussion of the cases below reveals, in few of the subcategories of redistricting case law can a clear "winner" be declared between rules and standards. Rather, each new case presents a challenge to the courts as to whether to pick the language of standards or rules from the prevailing precedent. Should the one-person, one-vote rule require strict population equality or should reasonable departures be allowed for particular state interests? Is the notion of the majority-minority status of a district (that is, whether it is more than 50 percent black or Hispanic) in some way dispositive under either section 2 or section 5 of the Voting Rights Act or does a more flexible rule apply? Or in the context of state constitutional provisions that require respect for political subdivision lines, should a state try to minimize the number of split counties or does such a constitutional provision represent a merely aesthetic aspiration regarding a plan's appearance? In the context of redistricting litigation, the challenge for the litigants is to recraft the precedent as more rule- or standard-like depending on which approach best suits their position.

Activism versus Restraint

When the Warren Court first decided to get involved in redistricting, the debate was phrased principally as one between proponents of judicial activism and judicial restraint. In his plurality opinion in *Colegrove* v. *Green* and then later as a dissenter in *Baker* v. *Carr*, Justice Felix Frankfurter repeatedly warned against judicial submergence in political thickets.[5] The liberals on the Court, such as Warren and Brennan, were activist in this realm, as they were with respect to other individual rights (criminal rights, privacy rights, and free speech rights, to name a few)—that is to say, they were more likely to use their power to strike down laws as unconstitutional. Despite having no originalist hook on which to hang judicial involvement in redistricting (let alone a right to vote, which the justices manufactured out of whole cloth), the activists prevailed, paving the way for later judicial involvement, even outside the context of malapportionment. With each additional foray into politics, however, one can see a similar (if not as heated) debate concerning whether judges should be involved in that new area.

The debate here sometimes parallels the rules-standards debate when the contemplated rule is one of nonjusticiability; in most cases, however, the debate falls along different lines drawn according to the judge's perception of the proper role of the judiciary in regulating politics. Of course, "activism" has now become an overused insult to be hurled at any judge whose decision one dislikes. Fundamentally, however, the analysis with respect to activism or restraint in the redistricting context mirrors concerns expressed in jurisprudence surrounding the political question doctrine, which (to oversimplify) asks whether there are good reasons for judges to leave the political branches alone when it comes to interpretation of a particular constitutional provision. Those reasons generally involve some conclusion that the issue is textually committed to another branch of government, that judicially administrable standards are nonexistent, or that judicial involvement would show disrespect for or overly intrude on another branch of government. Advocates of judicial restraint, like the framers of the Constitution, adhere closely to the notion that the judiciary should be the least dangerous of the three branches of government. Deference to legislatures should be the rule, and even when a constitutional provision is applicable, prudential considerations counsel strongly in favor of upholding a law unless compelling reasons suggest otherwise.

In contrast, judicial activists view the political realm as the paradigmatic context in which the judiciary should be aggressively involved. The famous footnote 4 of *United States* v. *Carolene Products Co.*,[6] upon which much of the Warren Court jurisprudence and its academic defense were intentionally or subconsciously based, suggested that judicial involvement was particularly appropriate to protect discrete and insular minorities or to police the electoral process when the channels of political change had become clogged.[7] Activists, then and now, view the Court as the only possible check when a majority tyrannizes a minority or when a minority captures the political process and immunizes itself from genuine political competition. In the redistricting context, evidence of the "discrete and insular minorities" strand might be seen in the race-based vote dilution cases, where a white majority enhanced its power at the expense of an African American minority. And the one-person, one-vote cases stand as the paradigmatic case for "representation reinforcement" since, absent the Court's intervention (the argument goes), incumbents elected from malapportioned districts never would have an incentive or desire to revamp the system in favor of equally populated districts. The judiciary, in this view, is perfectly situated to prevent incumbent foxes from guarding the electoral henhouse.

However, activism in the redistricting realm (let alone other areas of constitutional law) has not been limited to liberal defenders of the *Carolene Products* rationales. In the *Shaw* v. *Reno* line of cases, for example, conservatives discovered an "analytically distinct" claim in the equal protection clause that largely prevented states from drawing majority-minority districts in which race was the "predominant factor," meaning that race subordinated traditional districting principles.[8] Activism can sprout from textualism and norms of color blindness just as it can from liberal theories of fundamental fairness or individual rights. Activists are primarily distinguished by their willingness to strike down legislation and their lack of deference to the political branches, rather than by their adherence to any particular interpretive method.

Group Rights versus Individual Rights

The last interpretive dimension for the redistricting cases may be the most difficult to describe, but it is perhaps most illustrative of contemporary controversies. To some extent the group rights–individual rights dimension tracks political lines—as in controversies over multiculturalism and affirmative action—with conservatives opposing group rights and liberals embracing them, but the fit is not always so neat. At its core, the divergence between the two conceptions of the values at stake in the redistricting process is based on whether a given redistricting controversy is seen as affecting (or diluting) an individual's vote or as involving the underrepresentation of or discrimination against a particular group.

The groupist and individualist conceptions of the values at stake do not always lead to different results in redistricting cases. The one-person, one-vote cases, for example, express both types of values. On one hand, in *Reynolds* v. *Sims*, the Court emphasized that "rights allegedly impaired [by malapportionment] are individual and personal in nature."[9] "Legislators represent people, not trees or acres. Legislators are elected by voters, not farms or cities or economic interests." Concluding that malapportionment is tantamount to giving one voter ten votes while giving his neighbor only one, the Court emphasized that the "weight of a citizen's vote cannot be made to depend on where he lives" and "[t]o the extent that a citizen's right to vote is debased, he is that much less a citizen."

In the same opinion, however, the Court recognized the necessarily groupist implications of malapportionment: "[I]n a society ostensibly grounded on representative government, it would seem reasonable that a majority of the people of a State could elect a majority of that State's legislators." Moreover, just below the surface of the early opinions themselves lurked the basic controversy—that the static malapportioned legislatures overrepresented rural areas and underrepresented cities and suburbs. In other words, those cases were primarily about group power and representation as opposed to some tenuous connection to individual rights. (Indeed, the actual weight of an individual's vote is more a product of the competitiveness of a district than the number of people living in it: in other words, how valuable or powerful is one's vote in a district of any size if the winner of the election is preordained?)

When the Court turns its attention to redistricting as a means of representation, it focuses on representation of groups. As Justice Lewis Powell's separate opinion in *Davis* v. *Bandemer* explained: "[t]he concept of 'representation' necessarily applies to groups: groups of voters elect representatives, individual voters do not."[10] In cases under section 2 of the Voting Rights Act, for example, the inquiry is necessarily whether members of a particular group have an equal opportunity to elect their candidates of choice. The *Bandemer* standard for partisan gerrymandering cases was whether "the electoral system is arranged in a manner that will consistently degrade a voter's or a group of voters' influence on the political process as a whole" and thereby cause "continued frustration of the will of the majority of the voters or effective denial to a minority of voters of a fair chance to influence the political process."

The fault lines in *Shaw* v. *Reno* and its progeny also tend to fall along a group rights–individual rights dimension. Here, however, it is less clear whether the rule of law in *Shaw* itself grows out of a preference for individual over group rights or emerges from five justices' particular discomfort with the group-based (that is, excessively pro-minority) districts that the states created in those cases. The intentional creation of majority-minority districts, according to the *Shaw* majority, reinforces racial stereotypes and sends a message to representatives from those districts: "When a district obviously is created solely to effectuate the perceived common interests of one racial group, elected officials are more likely to believe that their primary obligation is to represent only the members of that group, rather than their constituency as a whole."[11] One difficulty with the *Shaw* opinions is that while they attack groupist gerrymandering, they fail to show that individual voters (minority or white, inside the gerrymandered district or outside) are injured by such gerrymanders.[12] While the cases themselves attack gerrymandering as a means to enforce group rights, their reliance on "expressive harms" (as Rick Pildes terms it[13]) necessarily presumes some kind of society-wide reception of a signal from such gerrymanders, rather than any particular individual injury.

The Redistricting Case Law: Where We Are and What We Have Done

With the terms of the assorted debates in redistricting law explained, this section turns to the case law to see what the Court has wrought, describing as briefly as possible the current state of the law in the various legal contexts and presenting the consequences to the degree that they can be measured. The basic "story" here, if there is one, is that the Court, with some help from Congress, has erected a massive superstructure of constraints on the redistricting process, many of which are in tension with one another. Each decision often has a significant short-term effect, but to a large extent actors then bargain around court-imposed constraints to achieve political motives that remain constant in the face of doctrinal change. Sometimes the Court softens the effect of its earlier pronouncements by converting rules into standards or hardens standards into rules to create greater predictability and stem the tide of potential litigation.

One Person, One Vote

THE LAW. The country first got into this mess, of course, when the Supreme Court decided that malapportioned districts could violate the equal protection clause. In *Baker* v. *Carr*, it appeared that something akin to rationality review would apply to district plans: in other words, states needed to find some justification for the lines that they drew, but perfect population equality would not be required. Later the Court clarified the one-person, one-vote rule to require substantial equality of population in noncongressional districts and population equality "to the extent practicable" for congressional districts. Departures from population equality can be justified, at least for noncongressional plans, to respect political subdivision lines and the cores of previous districts; to draw compact districts; and to avoid contests between incumbents. Until recently, many jurisdictions thought that the courts would look the other way in a noncongressional plan so long as the total deviation between districts did not exceed 10 percent. That dream of a safe harbor defined by a rigid percent threshold was rejected in 2004 in *Larios* v. *Cox*, when a federal district court (summarily affirmed by the Supreme Court) struck down the redistricting plans for the Georgia General Assembly despite the fact that their total deviation was less than 10 percent.[14] The court concluded that no legitimate justification underlay the deviations, only illegitimate motives, such as intent to give an advantage to Democratic incumbents while punishing Republicans or to favor some parts of the state at the expense of others.

To say that the one-person, one-vote rule requires either perfect or substantial population equality does not answer the question "equality of what?" Many possible denominators exist: people, citizens, voting-age population, eligible voters, or registered voters. In *Burns* v. *Richardson*, the Court upheld a redistricting plan based on equal numbers of registered voters.[15] However, in *Karcher* v. *Daggett*, the Court suggested, while striking down a 0.7 percent deviation in a congressional redistricting plan, that "[a]dopting any standard other than population equality, using the *best census data available* . . . would subtly erode the Constitution's ideal of equal representation" [emphasis added].[16] At the time jurisdictions redistrict, only voting-age population (VAP) and aggregate population data (along with race data) are available from the Census Bureau. However, with *Burns* still on the books, the question (academic though it may be, given every current jurisdiction's use of census data) of whether jurisdictions may comply with the one-person, one-vote rule while using something other than census aggregate population totals remains unanswered.

THE CONSEQUENCES. Early studies of the one-person, one-vote cases found few systematic policy effects.[17] Some, like Edward Tufte, argued that the reapportionment cases (or, more properly, the decennial redistricting that they ordered) contributed to the incumbency advantage and the vanishing of marginal districts (that is, districts in which the eventual victor won by a close margin).[18] Others disagreed, pointing out that marginal districts began to vanish much earlier,[19] that incumbents in redrawn districts were not safer than incumbents in others,[20] and that the unredistricted Senate enjoyed a similar rise in incumbency over the same period.[21] In the past few years, however, those who have turned back the clock and looked at the data have found some dramatic effects.

Gary Cox and Jonathan Katz's recent book, *Elbridge Gerry's Salamander*, argues that the one-person, one-vote cases (and perhaps more important, their initial enforcement by Democratic-leaning judges and their timing, during the 1964 Democratic landslide election) helped reduce the Republican bias in non-Southern congressional elections that existed into the 1960s and also gave rise to the vanishing marginal districts in congressional elections.[22] They point out that decennial redistricting now has allowed challengers to time their entry and incumbents to time their exits to coincide with the redistricting cycle. As a result, the incumbency advantage has grown because vulnerable incumbents resign and ambitious challengers bide their time, often for an open seat caused by redistricting.

Stephen Ansolabehere, Alan Gerber, and Jim Snyder have demonstrated that the one-person, one-vote cases enhanced representation of urban areas.[23] Rectification of the rural bias caused by static lines, which did not keep up in some states with nearly a century of population shifts, led to a greater number of representatives from urban areas. The authors also estimate serious public policy effects from the reduction of such a bias: specifically, the redistribution of approximately $7 billion to more populous counties. While they identify a shift in electoral power in favor of liberals, specifically on issues of civil rights, they do not find systematic partisan effects because the rural bias did not create a systematic advantage for one party across all fifty states.

Concerning the effect on state legislatures, my own work with Thad Kousser and Patrick Egan confirms the finding that the reapportionment revolution did not have systematic partisan effects.[24] However, in particular states the partisan effects were quite substantial. We also found that state houses and senates became more alike in terms of their partisan composition following the establishment of the one-person, one-vote rule, perhaps an unsurprising finding even if a new one. We found too that while legislatures were more likely to change hands in the first ten years following the first post-*Baker* redistricting, previously malapportioned legislatures were not more likely to change party control immediately following the redistricting than legislatures that were more equitably apportioned. Finally, in an attempt to prove a whimsical counterfactual, we overlaid the districting plans at issue in the four states on the *Reynolds* v. *Sims* docket onto current political data to figure out what might have happened had the ancient districts stayed in place. We found that in most cases such lines would have led to more accurate representation of the underlying partisan composition of the given electorate than do the current, equitably apportioned lines.

There are certainly other, less measurable effects that one can identify as flowing from the one-person, one-vote cases. The mere availability of the option of filing a claim allows partisan groups that lose in the political arena to try to take a second bite at the apple in court—for example, by successfully arguing that a deviation of seventeen people between Pennsylvania congressional districts violates the Constitution.[25] Courts, as a result, necessarily have waded further into the political thicket, sometimes drawing their own plans. The one-person, one-vote rule has also made electoral administration more difficult, as precinct boundaries need to be completely redrawn every ten years and the inevitable disrespect of political subdivision boundaries that results leads to voters being members of many different, noncoinciding jurisdictions at once. However, the chief consequence of the Court's intervention in the one-person, one-vote cases may be the reconceptualization of the judicial role as properly—and later increasingly—preoccupied with regulating the deep structures of U.S. elections.

Political Gerrymandering

THE LAW. In contrast to the sharp bite of the one-person, one-vote cases, the Supreme Court's regulation of partisan gerrymandering has been largely toothless. First in 1986 in *Davis* v. *Bandemer* and then in 2004 in *Vieth* v. *Jubelirer*, the Court failed to craft any meaningful restriction on partisan gerrymanders but at the same time never ruled out the possibility that somewhere down the road a redistricting plan might go over the constitutional line.[26] The debate among the justices centers largely on the idea of nonjusticiability due to the absence of administrable standards: because no clear line of demarcation exists to separate unconstitutional partisan gerrymanders from the "normal" use of partisanship in the redistricting process, a plurality of the Court in its most recent decision would have left the entire question of partisan gerrymandering to the political branches.

The standard for unconstitutional partisan gerrymanders that emerged from the plurality opinion in *Davis* v. *Bandemer* focused on discriminatory intent and effect. Legislatures were presumed to intend the partisan consequences of their redistricting plans. Discriminatory effect occurs if the "electoral system is arranged in a manner that will consistently degrade a voter's or a group of voters' influence on the political process as a whole. . . . [S]uch a finding of unconstitutionality must be supported by evidence of continued frustration of the will of a majority of voters or effective denial of a minority of voters of a fair chance to influence the political process."[27] The effect of such a standard was to create a partisan gerrymandering cause of action in name only, because no court could find a plan that met *Bandemer*'s high threshold. In upholding a Democratic gerrymander of California's congressional districts under *Bandemer*, one district court found it significant that 40 percent of the congressional delegation, one of the state's U.S. senators, and the sitting president at the time

(Ronald Reagan) were all California Republicans and that thus the Republicans were not "shut out" of the political process.[28]

The Supreme Court revisited the issue of partisan gerrymandering in 2004 in *Vieth* v. *Jubelirer*, which concerned a Republican gerrymander of Pennsylvania's congressional districts. The four-justice plurality opinion, written by Justice Scalia, who was joined by Justices O'Connor and Thomas and Chief Justice Rehnquist, would have overruled *Bandemer* and rejected the standards for unconstitutional gerrymandering proposed by the plaintiffs and any of the other justices. For those four, the issue of partisan gerrymandering presented a nonjusticiable political question due to the absence of any judicially manageable standard. The four more liberal justices (Stevens, Souter, Ginsburg, and Breyer) crafted three opinions emphasizing various standards and multifactor tests to rein in partisan gerrymanders, with some applying to challenges to individual districts and others to entire districting plans.

Justice Kennedy's opinion was the critical one in the case, however. He would not foreclose judicial review entirely, nor would he reverse or reaffirm *Davis* v. *Bandemer*, nor would he sign onto any of the standards proposed by the plaintiffs or the other justices. Nevertheless, he sided with the plurality in affirming the judgment of the district court, which upheld the gerrymander. While rejecting any of the proffered or existing standards, Justice Kennedy did not want to give up hope that such a standard might be discoverable in the future. He suggested that such a standard might be discoverable in the First Amendment, rather than in the equal protection clause, under which most right-to-vote and gerrymandering cases are litigated. For the same reason that the state cannot hire or fire employees on the basis of their political affiliation, the First Amendment may prevent the state from punishing voters on the basis of their party, he argued. "In the context of partisan gerrymandering . . . First Amendment concerns arise where an apportionment has the purpose and effect of burdening a group of voters' representational rights."[29] For now, it would appear that those who draw the lines are pretty much where they were before *Vieth*: while recognizing that a future Supreme Court majority might come up with a more aggressive standard, they can operate under the assumption that no court will strike down a partisan gerrymander.

Political gerrymandering is not always partisan, however. Politics can dominate the redistricting process without having lopsided partisan effects. The Court seems also to have given its blessing to bipartisan and incumbent-protecting gerrymanders, which often are not inconsistent with partisan gerrymanders, as the 2002 experience suggests. Bipartisan ger-rymanders divide a state into politically more homogeneous constituen-cies by creating districts that heavily favor either Democrats or Republi-cans. In *Gaffney* v. *Cummings*, the Supreme Court specifically permitted the drawing of districts that favored one party or the other, on the theory that proportional representation (that is, drawing lopsided districts that produce a delegation that accurately reflects the underlying partisan predisposition of the electorate) was a legitimate approach to redistricting.[30]

Incumbent-protecting gerrymanders, as their name suggests, consist of districts drawn to favor their respective incumbents. Although the Court has not dealt with a specific challenge to incumbent gerrymanders, in the one-person, one-vote cases, in the *Shaw* line of cases, and in several opinions in *Vieth*, the Court named incumbent protection as a legitimate state interest. Therefore, much to the chagrin of some legal theorists, the Court has not embraced an antitrust model of politics wherein its role would be to regulate the cartel-like behavior of entrenched parties or incumbents who try to insulate themselves from competition and make elections meaningless.[31]

THE CONSEQUENCES. As might be expected, the noninvolvement of the judiciary in policing political gerrymanders has led to politics domi-nating the process in most states. Thus, for states in which one party con-trols the redistricting process and stands to benefit from packing its oppo-nents and spreading its supporters more efficiently, partisan gerrymanders are frequent. In states where control of the redistricting process is divided, incumbent-protecting gerrymanders are the norm. Many see the effect of judicial noninvolvement in the bias of certain state legislatures or congres-sional delegations toward the party controlling the redistricting and in the lack of competitive congressional districts. Another frequently mentioned consequence is a rise in polarization due to the creation of more ideologi-cally homogeneous districts.

Sam Hirsch has demonstrated quite convincingly that, at least in the cur-rent round of redistricting, Republican control in competitive states has led to a Republican bias in congressional elections.[32] Of course, several states continue to have a Democratic bias in their redistricting plans, and many more had such a bias in the 1970s and 1980s, when a greater share of the population was Democratic and Democrats controlled a greater number of states. Nevertheless, as the recent Texas re-redistricting has demonstrated, judicial noninvolvement in this area has left majority parties with the feel-ing that they can redraw districts to their advantage with abandon.[33] And it seems a fair inference that political parties in control of the state legislative redistricting process may be better able (due to judicial noninvolvement and the effectiveness of partisan gerrymanders) to prevent control from changing hands.

With respect to bipartisan and incumbent-protecting gerrymanders, most observers argue that they have produced less competitive elections and increased polarization in the U.S. House of Representatives and state legislatures. I was probably the last holdout when it came to questioning the effect of gerrymandering on district-level competition.[34] However, the data on the level and location of noncompetitive elections in 2002 elections suggests that gerrymandering has had a more dramatic effect on intradistrict competition than it once did. Although those elections demonstrate that redistricting aided in creating noncompetitive districts for about 90 percent of the House of Representatives, one cannot ignore the fact that the unredistricted U.S. Senate continues to have incumbent reelection rates of close to 90 percent, so redistricting cannot be the principal cause of the low levels of incumbent defeats.

Others point to bipartisan gerrymanders as producing ideologically homogeneous districts and thus more legislators at the political extremes than at the center. The argument suggests that the median voter in a bipartisan gerrymandered district is far to the left or right of the median voter in the state or nation. As a result, the primary election becomes the dispositive election in such politically lopsided districts, and politicians who cater to such selected constituencies are more likely to be extreme as well. No doubt the parties in the legislature are farther apart from each other than they have been for perhaps a century, and they are also more internally cohesive—that is, the ideological distance between legislators of the same party is smaller than it once was. Is redistricting to blame?

I tend to think that the effect of redistricting on polarization has been overblown. The unredistricted Senate has seen a parallel rise in polarization over the same period. Also, it is not abundantly clear that representatives from ideologically homogeneous constituencies and those from more balanced ones are voting in markedly different ways. Organizational changes within the chambers have produced greater hierarchy within the congressional party caucuses, and centralized control of the parties' campaign money has allowed leaders to extort compliant behavior from members. Both of these phenomena are more responsible for polarization than is redistricting. Moreover, the electorate is more polarized and partisan as well, as measured by consistency in voting behavior and declines in split-ticket voting, even if one-third of the electorate continues to identify itself as independent. So a polarized legislature is not so surprising. At least in theory, however, such a relationship between bipartisan gerrymanders and polarization has intuitive appeal, even if the data may not yet demonstrate that such a relationship exists.

When trying to explain the renewed fervor and success of partisan gerrymandering, observers tend to point to new computer technology that allows redistricters to carve up jurisdictions into predictable voting blocs. However, the technology would be useless for that purpose if voting behavior were not becoming more predictable. Gerrymanders are successful because a line drawer can now count on voters (that is, census blocks and precincts) to behave in a particular way, whereas in previous redistricting cycles voters might routinely defy predictions. Although the tools used to redistrict have become more sophisticated, fundamentally a gerrymander is only as reliable as the voters it seeks to place into districts.

Racial Gerrymandering

THE LAW. Before *Shaw* v. *Reno*, racial gerrymandering usually referred to the use of the redistricting process to overrepresent the racial group in power and underrepresent the racial group out of power. The test for proving unconstitutional racial gerrymandering, as codified in *Mobile* v. *Bolden*, was the same as that for other violations of the equal protection clause: the plaintiff must prove discriminatory intent and effect. In other words, the plaintiff must show both that those in power were intentionally using the redistricting process to minimize the power of the plaintiff's racial group and that they succeeded in doing so.

Shaw v. *Reno* created an "analytically distinct claim" from the *Mobile* racial vote dilution claim based on the excessive use of race in creating a particular district. *Miller* v. *Johnson* clarified that so-called *Shaw* claims could arise when race was the "predominant factor" in the drawing of a district.[35] To prove a *Shaw* claim, plaintiffs who live in an allegedly unconstitutional district need to demonstrate that traditional redistricting principles—such as compactness, contiguity, respect for political subdivisions and communities of interest, and avoidance of incumbent pairings—were subordinated to race in the construction of a district. Once the plaintiff has demonstrated the predominant use of race, it falls to the state to prove that its use of race in the creation of the district in question was necessary to avoid a violation of the Voting Rights Act. In the likely event that it cannot do so, then a court will strike down the district as an unconstitutional racial gerrymander.

THE CONSEQUENCES. Perhaps the greatest effect of *Shaw* and its progeny has been environmental, due to the many forests that were razed to produce the volumes of law review criticism of these cases. Critics view *Shaw* as adhering to a racial double standard, as departing from normal rules of constitutional injury and standing, and as doctrinally incoherent. As a result of *Shaw*, redistricting plans in certain jurisdictions, such as North Carolina, spent much of the 1990s being whipsawed back and forth between the Supreme Court and lower courts. Most people predicted that the 2000 round would evince an avalanche of litigation due to the ambiguous and malleable *Shaw* standard, which seemed ripe for manipulation by partisan actors and likely to cause endless confusion in the courts. The floodgates never opened, however, and the Supreme Court has not even considered in any written opinion a single district from the 2000 round under *Shaw*.

Why was there no torrent of litigation? Although one cannot be completely sure why this dog didn't bark, there are several possible explanations. First, state legislatures drew fewer strangely shaped majority-minority districts. Although *Miller* v. *Johnson* held that shape was not essential in proving a *Shaw* claim, many jurisdictions operated on the (probably quite appropriate) assumption that squiggly minority districts were more likely to be struck down. As a result, many jurisdictions took the cue: if one needed to draw bizarre shapes to accomplish the varied purposes of a gerrymander, it was best to make the bizarre districts the largely white districts. The *Shaw-Miller* standard of racial predominance, despite its many ambiguities, also turned out not to be difficult to apply. Although the Court admonished that this was not an area regulated by "I-know-it-when-I-see-it" jurisprudence, most redistricting officials knew a *Shaw*-violative district when they saw it, so they found ways not to draw it.

Second, the push by the Department of Justice (DOJ), interest groups, and some politicians for the creation of majority-minority districts in the 1990 redistricting diminished considerably in the 2000 round. The DOJ precleared all congressional plans for the 2000 round, and as a result of some other Supreme Court decisions described below, DOJ did not have the legal authority to pursue a quasi-maximization strategy similar to that of the 1990s. Furthermore, the NAACP Legal Defense Fund, which was at the forefront of redistricting planning and litigation during the 1990s, did not vigorously participate in the drawing of maps and challenging of plans in the 2000 round. Because many heavily minority districts survived into the 2000 round, the minority elected officials from those districts could defend their own interests in the line-drawing process. In the 1990s, by contrast, only outside pressure led to the creation of safe minority seats. Also, as a result of suspicions and social science studies that suggested that the creation of super-majority-minority districts in the early 1990s contributed to the Republican takeover of the U.S. House of Representatives, minority elected officials (many of whom were elected pursuant to the intentional creation of their 1990 districts) were willing to give up some of their voters for the good of the Democratic Party. Now that they enjoyed incumbency advantages, more-over, those Democratic incumbents did not need overly concentrated minor-ity districts in order to be reelected, whereas such percentages may have been necessary to elect a minority candidate to an open seat. In the end, jurisdic-tions did not feel the internal or external pressure to maximize the number of majority-minority districts that they did ten years prior.

Finally, the last chapter in the story of the Supreme Court's microman-agement of North Carolina's congressional districts during the last round seemed to provide some cover for jurisdictions seeking to defend majority-minority districts. On the eve of the 2000 redistricting, the Supreme Court, in *Easley* v. *Cromartie*, finally upheld a set of North Carolina con-gressional districts for the 1990s.[36] Justice O'Connor joined the four more liberal justices to hold that the congressional district in question was pre-dominantly based on partisan considerations, not race, and therefore strict scrutiny was not triggered. In other words, if a majority-minority district (or "its functional equivalent," to quote a cryptic phrase from the last para-graph of the opinion) can be credibly described as a reliably Democratic district (and intentionally and predominantly drawn as such), then party, not race, "predominated" in its construction. As a result of *Easley*, then, the task for line drawers (and all those whose statements or intentions are potentially relevant in the face of a *Shaw* challenge) is to describe and demonstrate that minority voters are the most reliable Democrats and that heavily Democratic districts, which just so happen to be majority-minority, were drawn for partisan, not racial, reasons.

Section 5 of the Voting Rights Act

THE LAW. Section 5 of the Voting Rights Act requires certain covered jurisdictions to submit their redistricting plans for preclearance by the Department of Justice or the U.S. District Court for the District of

Columbia. Preclearance should be granted (and ordinarily is) so long as the redistricting plan does not have a retrogressive purpose or effect. Retrogression occurs when a redistricting plan makes minorities worse off than they were under the extant "benchmark" plan (that is, the last legally enforceable redistricting plan). The million-dollar question for retrogression analysis, then, is how do you know when a plan makes or intends to make a racial minority group worse off?

Retrogression does not mean discrimination. A jurisdiction can avoid retrogressing and still discriminate against a racial minority group: that is, a plan can both make minorities better off than they were before and still not give them the amount of representation that they warrant. Indeed, as the Court held in *Reno* v. *Bossier Parish I and II*, a districting plan can violate section 2 of the Voting Rights Act or can even be intentionally discriminatory without being retrogressive in purpose or effect.[37] Under section 5, desire or success in discriminating is not enough; the jurisdiction must actually intend to make minority voters worse off than before or succeed in doing so. DOJ must preclear even an illegal or unconstitutional plan so long as there is no backsliding in minority voting power.

The standard for what constitutes retrogression underwent a significant reformulation in 2003 in the Supreme Court's decision in *Georgia* v. *Ashcroft*. Before that, many may have thought, following *Beer* v. *United States*, that the section 5 retrogression inquiry concerned primarily the reduction in the number of majority-minority districts or perhaps significant reductions in the minority percentages within such districts.[38] *Georgia* v. *Ashcroft* established that a jurisdiction may offset a diminution in either the number of majority-minority districts or the minority percentages in those districts by creating districts in which minorities do not necessarily control the outcome but in which they have significant influence. From the opinion itself one does not really learn what constitutes a credible influence district; at different times the Court refers to districts that are 20 percent, 25 percent, and 30 percent black voting-age population. Of course, the percentage of minority voters needed in a district to ensure minority "influence" is a context-specific empirical question. The important lesson from the decision, however, is that section 5 does not reify *majority*-minority districts, per se, and that jurisdictions can choose between a greater number of districts in which minorities have influence and fewer districts in which they exercise control.

THE CONSEQUENCES. There can be no doubt that the Justice Department's aggressive enforcement of section 5 of the Voting Rights Act led to the election of an unprecedented number of African American and Hispanic representatives to the U.S. House of Representatives and state legislatures in the 1990s. Indeed, its aggressive enforcement also led to the reining in of the DOJ by *Georgia* v. *Ashcroft*, the *Bossier Parish* decisions, *Shaw* v. *Reno*, and their progeny. Moreover, the creation of these districts, many argue, accelerated the decline of the Democratic Party in the South and contributed to the Republican takeover of the U.S. House and several state legislatures as white Democratic representatives saw some of their most reliable partisans taken from their districts. In a dramatic revisionist (and I believe untrue) writing of history, some observers now speculate that an unholy alliance of Republicans, the George H. W. Bush Justice Department, and racial minorities forced the creation of pro-minority but anti–Democratic Party districting plans in the 1990s. Some continue to level similar charges of partisanship infecting preclearance review to this day, suggesting that in a rare exercise of its preclearance authority, the Ashcroft Justice Department asked for more information on a Mississippi congressional plan, with the result that a federal court plan favoring Republicans then went into effect.

In sum, there can be no doubt that the unique statutory scheme of section 5, with its remarkable intrusion on state sovereignty, has had the intended effect of securing at least descriptive and perhaps substantive representation for racial and language minorities. *Georgia* v. *Ashcroft* defangs section 5 considerably, however, and it is too early to tell whether the effect will be the intended flexibility in dealing with apportionment plans that sacrifice control for genuine influence or the unintended effect of looking the other way when state legislatures break up minority districts into substantial but ultimately uninfluential 20 percent or 30 percent districts. If the Texas re-redistricting is any indication of the future, covered jurisdictions controlled by Republicans are likely to continue to adhere to the *Beer* standard (which remains a valid option after *Ashcroft*) and to make heavily minority districts the only safe Democratic districts. Democratic jurisdictions, on the other hand, will take advantage of *Ashcroft* and try to spread their most reliable supporters most efficiently to retain as many seats as possible. DOJ, which has been relatively silent this go round, may be even more muted next time, now that covered jurisdictions have a larger buffet of redistricting options from which to choose in order to avoid retrogression.

Section 2 of the Voting Rights Act

THE LAW. Minority vote dilution can occur either through overconcentration of the minority community into a few districts (packing), excessive dispersion (cracking) of the minority community among too many districts, or submergence of a minority in a multimember district (stacking). Congress amended section 2 of the Voting Rights Act in 1983 to eliminate the intent requirement set forth in *Mobile* v. *Bolden* and to replace it with a pure effects test. The earliest cases brought under section 2 (like *Bolden* itself) targeted multimember, at-large schemes that submerged a minority community (stacking) in such a way that it could not elect a single member of a local governing body, for example. In *Thornburgh* v. *Gingles*, the Court attempted to synthesize or winnow down the various "Senate Factors" behind the 1983 VRA amendments and established a three-pronged test for challenges to such multimember districts:[39]

(1) Is the minority community sufficiently large and geographically compact to constitute a majority in a single member district?
(2) Is the minority politically cohesive?
(3) And does the white majority vote consistently as a bloc to enable it usually to defeat the minority's preferred candidate at the polls?

I think it is fair to say that the subsequent lower-court cases implementing the *Gingles* "prongs" have failed to agree on some important definitions of what each prong means (and I admit to glossing over large swaths of case law here); nevertheless, throughout the 1980s and 1990s, courts forced the creation of majority-minority districts in most jurisdictions where plaintiffs requested such districts and met the *Gingles* criteria.[40]

Johnson v. *De Grandy* attempted to clarify whether the satisfaction of the *Gingles* conditions was necessary, sufficient, or both when plaintiffs were challenging not multimember districts that completely shut them out of the political process but single-member districting schemes that allegedly underrepresented the plaintiffs' minority group.[41] From *De Grandy* came an additional wrinkle—that proof of the *Gingles* factors alone might not be sufficient to show illegal vote dilution in a single-member districting scheme. In particular, evidence that the share of majority-minority districts in the jurisdiction was roughly proportional to the minority's share of the population is a factor counseling against a finding of a violation of section 2. As the *DeGrandy* Court added, failure to maximize the number of majority-minority districts cannot define a section 2 violation.

Among the many important lingering questions surrounding section 2 is the relevance of influence districts, either as a shield against such claims or as a sword to force their creation. As a shield against a section 2 claim, a jurisdiction might argue, as did New Jersey in *Page* v. *Bartels*, that the creation of a majority African American or majority Hispanic district is unnecessary (and would perhaps reduce minority voting power) given the number of effective influence districts that exist under the plan.[42] Such an argument fits within *Gingles* itself, in that the implication is that such influence districts "work" because voters are willing to cross over or form coalitions with the members of the protected class. The more interesting question is whether, despite *Gingles*'s emphasis on majority-minority districts, minorities can sue for the creation of an influence district, however one defines it.[43] Contrary to other courts that have entertained this question, the First Circuit recently said yes in *Metts* v. *Murphy*, but emphasized that the hurdles were high; it would not be easy for a group to show both that racial bloc voting prevented it from electing its candidates of choice and that an influence district was at the same time a necessary and effective way of ensuring that minorities had an equal opportunity to elect their candidates of choice.[44]

THE CONSEQUENCES. There is much more to say on the morass of section 2 litigation. Alongside section 5, section 2 led to the widespread elimination of dilutive at-large voting systems, to the creation of a large number of majority-minority districts, and to the election of a record number of minority representatives, particularly in local and state legislative bodies. Critics of section 2, like those of section 5, argue it led to the creation of racial fiefdoms or that it hurt the Democratic Party. To overgeneralize, however, I think it is fair to say that, as with many of the other claims mentioned thus far, the political parties have hijacked section 2 and turned it into one more weapon in their arsenal to attack plans that put them at a political disadvantage. To be sure, several "genuine" section 2 claims often present themselves, but the newest cases primarily represent attempts by losers in the political process to take a second bite at the redistricting apple. Thus, when Republicans felt shafted by the New Jersey legislative plan, they alleged dilution of African American and Hispanic votes, and the Democrats, incensed by the Republican gerrymander in the Texas re-redistricting, said the same thing. Fundamentally, however, those were political fights being waged through the dangerous proxy of race-based arguments in court. To be sure, the mere fact that a gerrymander is partisan does not immunize it from the effects test of section 2, as it might a *Shaw* claim per *Easley*, for example. However, everyone should be concerned by the necessarily poisonous rhetoric that seeks to tag partisan gerrymanders as racist, when in reality they are merely greedy attempts to undermine democracy, inhibit competition, and misrepresent communities.

Conclusions

The state of the law for those who draw redistricting plans is as follows. The plans that they draw must abide by the rule of population equality, but in some cases they might be able to depart from it depending on the legitimacy and authenticity of their reasons for doing so. Also, they must make sure that they do not overly concentrate (pack) or overly disperse (crack) minority communities, or they may run afoul of the Voting Rights Act. And while paying great attention to race as they attempt to navigate between the twin dangers of packing and cracking, they must make sure that race does not become the predominant factor in the creation of a district. Of course, in the event that they are charged with using race predominantly, they must be prepared to say that the Voting Rights Act made them do it or, alternatively and contradictorily, that their primary intent was partisanship all the while and compliance with the Voting Rights Act was, well, pleasantly inadvertent. Of course, they should beware of choosing the latter route because in a nearby thicket lies the Supreme Court, perhaps with a new rule against partisan gerrymandering that will force them back to the drawing board.

Notes

1. See, for example, Kathleen M. Sullivan, "The Justices of Rules and Standards," *Harvard Law Review* 106 (1992): 22; Carol M. Rose, "Crystals and Mud in Property Law," *Stanford Law Review* 40 (1988): 577, 590–93; Cass R. Sunstein, "Problems with Rules," *California Law Review* 83 (1995): 953; Pierre Schlag, "Rules and Standards," *UCLA Law Review* 33 (1985): 379–430.

2. *Davis* v. *Bandemer*, 478 U.S. 109 (1986).

3. *Whitcomb* v. *Chavis*, 403 U.S. 124 (1971); *White* v. *Regester*, 412 U.S. 755 (1973); *Mobile* v. *Bolden*, 446 U.S. 55.

4. *Georgia* v. *Ashcroft*, 539 U.S. 461 (2003).

5. *Colegrove* v. *Green*, 328 U.S. 549 (1946); *Baker* v. *Carr*, 369 U.S. 186 (1962).

6. *United States* v. *Carolene Products Co.*, 304 U.S. 144, 153 n. 4 (1938).

7. John Hart Ely, *Democracy and Distrust: A Theory of Judicial Review* (Harvard University Press, 1980), pp. 105–34.

8. *Shaw* v. *Reno*, 509 U.S. 630 (1993).

9. *Reynolds* v. *Sims*, 377 U.S. 533 (1964).

10. *Davis* v. *Bandemer*, 478 U.S. 109, 167 (1986) (Justice Powell concurring in part and dissenting in part).

11. *Shaw*, 509 U.S. 630, 649.

12. See, generally, Samuel Issacharoff and Pamela S. Karlan, "Standing and Misunderstanding in Voting Rights Law," *Harvard Law Review* 111 (1998): 2276, 2279–87.

13. Richard H. Pildes and Richard G. Niemi, "Expressive Harms, 'Bizarre Districts,' and Voting Rights: Evaluating Election-District Appearances after *Shaw* v. *Reno,*" *Michigan Law Review* 92 (1993): 483.

14. *Larios* v. *Cox,* 300 F. Supp.2d 1320 (N.D. Ga. 2004), *summ. aff'd* 124 S. Ct. 2806 (2004).

15. *Burns* v. *Richardson,* 384 U.S. 73 (1966).

16. *Karcher* v. *Daggett,* 462 U.S. 725 (1983).

17. Those that found little public policy change include Herbert Jacob, "The Consequences of Malapportionment: A Note of Caution," *Social Force* 43 (December 1964): 256–61; Thomas Dye, "Malapportionment and Public Policy in the States," *Journal of Politics* 27 (August 1965): 586–601; Richard Hofferbert, "The Relation between Public Policy and Some Structural and Environmental Variables in the American States,"*American Political Science Review* 60 (March 1966): 73–82; David Brady and Douglas Edmonds, "One Man, One Vote—So What?" *Transaction* 4 (1967): 941; Bryan R. Fry and Richard F. Winters, "The Politics of Redistribution," *American Political Science Review* 64 (1970): 508; Robert Erikson, "Reapportionment and Policy: A Further Look at Some Intervening Variables," *Annals of the New York Academy of Sciences* 219 (1973): 280; and William E. Bicker, "The Effects of Malapportionment in the States—A Mistrial," in *Reapportionment in the 1970s,* edited by Nelson W. Polsby (University of California Press, 1971), critiquing the relevant literature. Those finding minor policy effects include Allan Pulsipher and James Weatherby, "Malapportionment, Party Competition, and the Functional Distribution of Governmental Expenditures," *American Political Science Review* 62 (1968): 1207; Roger A. Hanson and Robert E. Crew Jr., "The Policy Impact of Reapportionment," *Law and Society Review* 8 (1973): 69; H. George Frederickson and Yong Hyo Cho, "Legislative Apportionment and Fiscal Policy in the American States," *Western Political Quarterly* 27 (1974): 5.

18. See Edward R. Tufte, "The Relationship between Seats and Votes in Two-Party Systems," *American Political Science Review* 67 (1973): 551–53. See also Robert S. Erikson, "The Partisan Impact of State Legislative Reapportionment," *Midwest Journal of Political Science* 15 (1971): 57; Robert S. Erikson, "Malapportionment, Gerrymandering, and Party Fortunes in Congressional Elections," *American Political Science Review* 66 (1972): 1234; Gallagher and Weschler, "California," in *Impact of Reapportionment on the Thirteen Western States,* edited by E. Bushnell (University of Utah Press, 1970), p. 86; Albert D. Cover and David R. Mayhew, "Congressional Dynamics and the Decline of Competitive Congressional Elections," in *Congress Reconsidered,* 2d. ed., edited by Lawrence C. Dodd and Bruce C. Oppenheimer (Washington: Congressional Quarterly Press, 1981); Richard Born, "Generational Replacement and the Growth of Incumbent Reelection Margins in the U.S. House," *American Political Science Review* 73 (1979): 811; James L. Payne, "The Personal Electoral Advantage of House Incumbents, 1936–1976," *American Political Quarterly* 8 (1980): 465; Charles S. Bullock III, "Redistricting and Congressional Stability," *Journal of Politics* 37 (1975): 569.

19. See James C. Garand and Donald A. Gross, "Changes in the Vote Margins for Congressional Candidates: A Specification of Historical Trends," *American Political Science Review* 78 (1984): 17; Walter Dean Burnham, *Critical Elections and the Mainsprings of American Politics* (New York: Norton, 1970); Donald A. Gross and James C. Garand, "The Vanishing Marginals: 1824–1980," *Journal of Politics* 46 (1984): 227.

20. John A. Ferejohn, "On the Decline of Competition in Congressional Elections," *American Political Science Review* 71 (1977): 166; Bullock, "Redistricting and Congressional Stability"; Albert D. Cover, "One Good Term Deserves Another: The Advantage of Incumbency in Congressional Elections," *American Journal of Political Science* 21 (1977): 523.

21. Warren Lee Kostroski, "Party and Incumbency in Post-War Senate Elections: Trends, Patterns and Models," *American Political Science Review* 67 (1973): 1213. See also Benjamin Highton, "Senate Elections in the United States, 1920–94," *British Journal of Political Science* 30 (2000): 483; Michael

Krashinsky and William J. Milne, "The Effects of Incumbency in U.S. Congressional Elections, 1950–1988," *Legal Studies Quarterly* 18 (1993): 321.

22. Gary W. Cox and Jonathan M. Katz, *Elbridge Gerry's Salamander: The Electoral Consequences of the Reapportionment Revolution* (Cambridge University Press, 2002).

23. Stephen Ansolabehere, Alan Gerber, and James M. Snyder Jr., "Equal Votes, Equal Money: Court-Ordered Redistricting and Public Expenditures in the American States," *American Political Science Review* 96 (2002): 767; Stephen Ansolabehere and James M. Snyder Jr., "Reapportionment and Party Realignment in the American States," *University of Pennsylvania Law Review* 153 (November 2004). See also Mathew D. McCubbins and Thomas Schwartz, "Congress, the Courts, and Public Policy: Consequences of the One Man, One Vote Rule," *American Journal of Political Science* 32 (1988): 388, finding that congressional ballot allocations were less biased in favor of rural areas after 1964.

24. Nathaniel Persily, Thad Kousser, and Patrick Egan, "The Complicated Impact of One Person, One Vote on Political Competition and Representation," *North Carolina Law Review* 80 (2002): 1299.

25. *Vieth v. Pennsylvania*, 195 F. Supp. 2d 672 (M.D. Pa. 2002).

26. *Vieth v. Jubelirer*, 124 S. Ct. 1769 (2004).

27. *Davis v. Bandemer*, 478 U.S. 109, 132 (1986), plurality opinion.

28. *Badham v. Eu*, 694 F. Supp. 664, 670 (N.D. Cal. 1988) (three-judge court), *summarily aff'd*, 488 U.S. 1024 (1989).

29. *Vieth v. Jubelirer*, 124 S. Ct. at 1797.

30. *Gaffney v. Cummings*, 412 U.S. 735 (1973).

31. Samuel Issacharoff, "Gerrymandering and Political Cartels," *Harvard Law Review* 116 (2002): 593.

32. See Sam Hirsch, "The United States House of Unrepresentatives: What Went Wrong in the Latest Round of Congressional Redistricting," *Election Law Journal* 2 (2003): 179.

33. *Session v. Perry*, 298 F. Supp. 2d 451 (E.D. Tex. 2004) (per curiam).

34. See Nathaniel Persily, "In Defense of Foxes Guarding Henhouses: The Case for Judicial Acquiescence to Incumbent-Protecting Gerrymanders," *Harvard Law Review* 116 (2002): 649–83.

35. *Miller v. Johnson*, 515 U.S. 900 (1995).

36. *Easley v. Cromartie*, 532 U.S. 234 (2001).

37. *Reno v. Bossier Parish I and II*, 520 U.S. 471 (1997).

38. *Beer v. United States*, 425 U.S. 130 (1976).

39. *Thornburgh v. Gingles*, 478 U.S. 30 (1986).

40. For a review of those questions and the relevant case law, see J. Gerald Hebert and others, *The Realists' Guide to Redistricting: Avoiding the Legal Pitfalls* (Chicago: American Bar Association, 2000), pp. 25–49.

41. *Johnson v. De Grandy*, 512 U.S. 997 (1994).

42. *Page v. Bartels*, 248 F.3d 175 (3d Cir. 2001).

43. In a much overlooked footnote in *Gingles*, however, the Court was careful not to foreclose the possibility that claims could be brought by some groups that did not constitute a numerical majority in a hypothetical single-member district.

44. *Metts v. Murphy*, 363 F.3d 8 (1st Cir. 2004).

5 Redistricting Reform: What Is Desirable? Possible?

Thomas E. Mann

The legitimacy of the American electoral system requires some minimal level of adherence to the principles of fairness, responsiveness, and accountability. Recent elections to the U.S. House of Representatives threaten those principles. Congressional contests suffer from an unusually high degree of incumbent safety, a precipitous decline in competitiveness, growing ideological polarization, and a fierce struggle between the major parties to manipulate the rules of the game to achieve, maintain, or enlarge majority control of the chamber. The spectacle of the Texas Republicans' successful mid-decade partisan gerrymander, which violated a century-long norm against undertaking more than one round of redistricting after each decennial census and threatened an arms race between the parties to reverse recently approved plans, elevated redistricting to the position of prime suspect in producing these maladies in American democracy.

Special thanks to Alan Murphy and Rob Wooley, who were instrumental in organizing the joint Brookings Institution–Institute of Governmental Studies conference at which the arguments in this and the other chapters were first presented; to Jennifer Mattingley, who helped extensively with the redistricting case studies; and again to Alan Murphy, for his research assistance on this chapter.

Earlier chapters in this volume weigh the evidence supporting and refuting that charge. And the evidence indicates that redistricting has contributed to the advantage of incumbents, the decline of competition, partisan bias, and the ideological polarization of the parties in Congress, although it is by no means the sole or even the most important factor in producing those outcomes. New technology and increased party-line voting have enhanced the capacity of those who redraw district lines to achieve their political objectives, but the same factors can also help others to frustrate achievement of those objectives. The Supreme Court's almost exclusive focus on equal population and racial gerrymandering has liberated as much as constrained the self-interested behavior of politicians and parties, yet a judicial plunge into the political thicket of partisan and bipartisan gerrymandering might be even more problematic.

This chapter considers the desirability and possibility of reducing the dominance of self-interested political actors in the redistricting process. Many practitioners and scholars are deeply skeptical of the whole idea of redistricting reform. Some of that skepticism is based on what they see as relatively weak evidence of the impact of redistricting on competition and partisanship. The redistricting ambitions of political actors have a muted effect, constrained as they are by geography, conflicting values and principles, competing interests, uncertain outcomes, and self-policing mechanisms. But mostly the skepticism is a consequence of an overwhelming sense that any efforts to replace the dominant American style of redistricting by legislative bodies with more neutral procedures and principles are unlikely to be successful and, even if adopted, are doomed to fail.

The United States is clearly an outlier in the democratic world when it comes to the role that politicians play in shaping the rules that affect their electoral future.[1] This particular manifestation of American exceptionalism extends well beyond the realm of legislative redistricting. Elections are administered and campaign finance laws enforced in highly partisan environments, with relatively little delegation to professional bureaucrats or nonpartisan bodies. The design of our Madisonian system is predicated on the assumption that political actors will inevitably act in their own interests. Rather than deny that self-interested behavior, the system is designed to employ a pluralistic interest group environment and the proper political institutions to channel it in ways that serve broader public goals. Suspicion of authority, political control of bureaucrats, decentralization, parochialism, and a highly contentious and politicized judicial process are all deeply embedded features of that system. The electoral rules of the game are subject to the same pluralistic struggle for power as elections and public policies.[2] Many believe that attempts to alter this reality are futile.

This *realpolitik* perspective on American politics has not been uniformly embraced. Recoiling from the self-dealing of politicians, early twentieth-century Progressives championed a broad reform agenda ranging from initiatives, party primaries, and nonpartisan elections to regulation of corporations and civil service reform. While much of their agenda was adopted and survives to this day, it has been criticized by historians and political scientists for strengthening the middle class at the expense of the working class and for promising more ethical behavior than it could deliver. The fault line between Madisonians and Progressives—or, in the parlance of party politics, between regulars and reformers—has reemerged in contemporary debates about political reform. For example, critics of campaign finance regulation wax eloquent about the futility of restricting the flow of money in politics and the infamous "law of unintended consequences." Supporters of such regulation, on the other hand, often invoke the values and rhetoric of their Progressive predecessors.

Unfortunately, the contentious debate about the efficacy of political reform fits all too well the current era of American politics, which is characterized by intense partisanship and ideological polarization of parties. Americans appear to have an unbounded capacity to speak past one another, pursuing with conviction and passion what E. J. Dionne Jr. has called "a politics dominated by false choices and phony issues."[3] Yet in reality regulars and reformers need not and sometimes do not inhabit sharply opposing camps. *Realpolitik* considerations are appropriately central to calculations of the costs and benefits of reform proposals and of the feasibility of their adoption. At the same time, a largely unregulated political marketplace can suffer from failures and underinvestment in valued goods just as an economic market can. Self-dealing by corporate executives is subject to aggressive, if not always successful, preventive and punitive legal measures; it is not naive to entertain comparable steps in the political arena.

During the most recent round of campaign finance reform, a number of political scientists who long considered themselves party regulars became strong advocates of legislation to restrict party soft money and regulate electioneering communications.[4] They argued that carefully crafted regulation of money in politics could achieve limited objectives and that strong parties are not incompatible with limits on the sources of party financing. To be sure, not all political scientists agreed.[5] It will take some time to assess the consequences of the new campaign finance law, but early indicators suggest that the political parties are adapting well in complying with it.[6]

Redistricting reform, then, should not be dismissed out of hand as incompatible with American politics. Powerful theoretical arguments, rooted in the principles and values of the U.S. system, have been advanced for alternatives to legislative control of redistricting. Dennis Thompson demonstrates how a proper understanding of popular sovereignty provides a compelling basis for independent judgment on redistricting decisions. In his view, legislative control prevents present majorities from escaping the "dead hand of past majorities."[7] Others make a more empirically based argument: that traditional redistricting practices are producing (or contributing significantly to) harmful consequences for the U.S. electoral system.[8] Moreover, some states have departed from traditional redistricting practices, providing both a prima facie case that alternatives are not merely fanciful conceptions of naïve reformers and a basis for drawing lessons from the alternative mechanisms adopted.

This chapter considers a range of alternatives to current practices in congressional redistricting. Conceptually, they can be classified in terms of what aspect of the redistricting process is altered and the means by which the alterations are achieved.[9] The former include the structure of the electoral system, the standards by which new maps are drawn, and the procedures used to create and approve new district boundaries. The latter entail constitutional, statutory, or judicial actions at the federal or state level.

Electoral System

Redrawing district boundaries is particularly problematic in an electoral system that has single-member districts. Multimember districts would reduce the importance of boundaries and thereby the incentive for political actors to manipulate the line-drawing process to serve their own interests. Nevertheless, some residual importance for redistricting could remain in multimember districts, depending on their size, the number of representatives in each district, and the rules under which the representatives are elected. If an explicitly proportional representation system was adopted, one with party lists or German-style compensation schemes for district outcomes that depart from proportionality, redistricting would become in effect a nonpolitical issue.[10]

No constitutional impediment prevents adoption of alternatives to the single-member-district, first-past-the-post system for electing members to the U.S. House of Representatives (assuming such alternatives worked within the decennial apportionment of House seats to the states). Until 1842, Congress left to the states the means by which they elected their

U.S. representatives. Some states used multimember districts and at-large elections, although most followed the practice of electing one member per district.[11] Then, in 1842, Congress enacted a law that required contiguous single-member congressional districts.[12] While that single-member standard was effectively repealed by the 1929 Congressional Reapportionment Act,[13] which omitted all uniform standards that states were to follow in redrawing House district lines, Congress in 1967 again passed a law requiring single-member congressional districts.[14] That statute remains in effect today.

Are the alleged problems associated with redistricting—incumbent protection, noncompetitive elections, and ideological polarization—sufficiently severe to justify adopting some form of proportional representation (PR) for House elections or giving states the option of enacting PR systems? Since the strengths and weaknesses of PR systems extend well beyond the issues associated with redistricting, any consideration of this alternative must perforce include topics such as government stability, minority representation, the role of minor parties, and presidential selection rules.[15] I suspect that Americans are some time away from beginning a serious conversation about proportional representation at the federal level, much less resolving the issue. New PR initiatives at the state and local level, however, may provide useful experience and familiarity with this alternative.

A less ambitious change in the structure of the electoral system involves some variant of the Louisiana model of an all-party primary in the general election followed by a runoff between the top two finishers if no candidate attracts more than 50 percent of the vote. Reformers have suggested the use of instant runoff voting (IRV) to eliminate the need for a second round of elections.[16] Combining the all-party primary with IRV is advanced primarily as a way of diminishing the ideological polarization of the parties. Candidates in an open, all-party primary, it is argued, would have less incentive to appeal to their party's core (and more ideologically extreme) supporters than in the present system. It is not at all clear, however, whether and how such an electoral system would reduce the incumbent advantage or increase the number of competitive seats. Nor can its impact on the larger party system be predicted with confidence.

Redistricting Standards

There is a long history of efforts at the federal and the state level to constrain the choices of congressional district mapmakers by imposing redistricting standards. Between 1842 and 1929, Congress established various national standards for congressional redistricting, including contiguity, compactness, and equality of population.[17] Out of that experience came the widely accepted view that Congress has the constitutional authority to impose on the states national standards governing congressional redistricting. That experience also demonstrated that states could ignore those standards with impunity. With the exception of the single-member district requirement, the standards appear to have had only a limited impact, if any, on the size and shape of districts. Congress's minimal influence on redistricting may have stemmed from its limited means to enforce the standards. The only enforcement power available to it was to refuse to seat members elected in districts drawn in violation of the standards, a serious step that no Congress was willing to take.[18]

Since 1929, many proposals for setting national redistricting standards have been offered, but, with the voting rights exception discussed below, none have survived the legislative process. Proposed standards have ranged from contiguity, compactness, equal population, adherence to local political boundaries, and respect for communities of interest to neutrality with regard to any political party or candidate.[19] The latter was of course designed to counter partisan and incumbent-protecting gerrymandering. Today, the one national standard that has attracted attention in Congress would prohibit more than a single round of congressional redistricting after the decennial apportionment. Of course, as long as Representative Tom DeLay, the chief architect of the Texas redistricting plan, remains majority leader, implementing such a prohibition will prove nearly impossible. The more interesting question is how a Democratic majority in Congress might react to the proposal.

One federal mandate regarding redistricting by states—the prohibition against minority vote dilution—has its roots in the Voting Rights Act (VRA) of 1965 and subsequent amendments, but the courts have taken the lead in fleshing out its application in the redistricting arena. Over time their jurisprudence has evolved from maximizing the number of majority-minority districts to prohibiting the use of race as the predominant factor in redistricting to sanctioning the creation of minority-influence districts.[20]

Another federal mandate—the requirement for equal population districts—is entirely a creature of the courts. In a series of decisions from *Wesberry* v. *Sanders* (1964) to *Karcher* v. *Daggett* (1983), the Supreme Court developed a standard of absolute population equality in determining whether a congressional redistricting plan is constitutional. Any departure from precise mathematical equality of district populations within states must be justified by some compelling state interest. While the equal population standard has eliminated the gross disparities associated with malapportioned districts and has constrained somewhat the ability of politicians to rig electoral outcomes, it has also provided an excuse and a cover for mapmakers seeking to extract every possible benefit from partisan and bipartisan gerrymanders. Easing somewhat the equal population standard (which is unlikely to do much damage to any reasonable conception of equal representation) might actually reduce the level of mischief by allowing more stability in district composition and respect for local political and social boundaries.[21]

In *Davis* v. *Bandemer* (1986) the Court appeared to be moving toward the imposition of another standard when it ruled that partisan gerrymandering is justiciable under the Constitution's equal protection clause. Yet by setting a high threshold for successful challenges—"evidence of continued frustration of the will of a majority of the voters or effective denial to a minority of voters of a fair chance to influence the political process"—the Court rendered this standard ineffectual. Only one successful partisan gerrymandering claim—in a judicial election—has been litigated under *Bandemer*.[22] The Court returned to this question in a case brought by Pennsylvania Democrats based on a map drawn for the 2002 elections. Its decision in *Vieth* v. *Jubelirer* (2004) appears to have maintained the status quo. Although all nine justices acknowledged that partisan gerrymandering could be unconstitutional, in rejecting the challenge the majority despaired of finding workable standards for determining the conditions under which it would be.[23] While litigation challenging the Texas mid-decade redistricting plan continues,[24] the federal courts do not appear to be a promising venue for reform.[25]

While *Vieth* deals exclusively with partisan gerrymandering, some legal scholars look to the courts to constrain what they see as more problematic—bipartisan, incumbent-protecting gerrymanders.[26] Others argue against any further judicial intervention to counter bipartisan or partisan gerrymanders.[27] In the past the Court has sanctioned the protection of incumbency as a legitimate redistricting objective,[28] so it is not easy to see how the Court might reverse itself now.[29]

On the state level, redistricting standards for congressional and state legislative mapmaking may be written into constitutions or codified by statute. The most common are equal population, VRA compliance, contiguity, compactness, adherence to existing political and geographical boundaries, and respect for communities of interest.[30] The logic of these largely aesthetic criteria is that they are both desirable in their own right and likely to constrain partisan and incumbent gerrymandering. Contiguity is the only standard that is almost universally applied (assuming that one accepts that two land masses joined by a body of water or a point are contiguous). The others more nearly represent general values to be sought rather than strict standards to be met. They often suffer from ambiguity (for example, how to define "compactness") and conflict with other standards. Compactness can work against natural communities of interest, especially racial minorities, and existing political boundaries; it can also have a disparate partisan effect. The equal population standard often requires mapmakers to split existing political and geographical communities.

A few states—Iowa, Washington, and Arizona—have adopted more explicitly political standards for redistricting. Mapmakers might be instructed to avoid favoring incumbent officeholders or one political party over another. This might be done by blind procedures—denying them certain information (election data or the location of incumbents' homes)—or by requiring them to draw districts that are demonstrably competitive or that treat both parties "fairly." Each of these approaches has its own set of complications, and they too can lead to conflicting standards.[31] Protecting racial and ethnic minorities, an overriding federal requirement, can reduce the number of competitive seats and diminish the responsiveness of legislative elections to shifts in public sentiment.

Redistricting Procedures

Congressional redistricting plans typically are drawn and approved through the normal state legislative process. Controlling both chambers of the legislature (or one in unicameral Nebraska) and the governorship gives a political party an enormous advantage in crafting a plan that advances its partisan interests. Split-party control, on the other hand, tends to reduce opportunities for partisan gains within states and to facilitate bipartisan gerrymanders.[32] It is no surprise that the national parties invest substantial resources in state legislative and gubernatorial elections leading up to each decennial reapportionment. However, such investment is no longer limited to those elections. Under the direction of Tom DeLay, Republicans mounted a full-scale campaign to gain control of the Texas House in the 2002 elections. Aided by a favorable legislative redistricting plan, their success gave the party unified control of the state government and thereby the means for crafting a partisan gerrymander of congressional districts that replaced the maps drawn by the courts two years earlier.

To be sure, unified party control of a state government is no guarantee of partisan gains.[33] Many states are too small or too homogeneous or both to produce such opportunities. Parties in other states are constrained by intraparty differences, the perceived risks to majority party incumbents from maximizing partisan gains, and the geographical distribution of state residents. For example, although Democrats dominated California government at the time of the post-2000 congressional redistricting, they chose to consolidate their gains in the previous election and engage in a bipartisan incumbent gerrymander with the minority Republicans.

Some states require supermajority approval of redistricting plans by the legislature, thus producing in most cases a political dynamic similar to split-party control of state government. Partisan plans are avoided but not without a cost to competition. Under such conditions, the highest priority of both parties is protecting their incumbents.

Since the reapportionment revolution of the 1960s, the courts have played an increasingly important role in the redistricting process. Before the Supreme Court imposed the "one person, one vote" standard on redistricting, failure to produce a new redistricting plan usually resulted in the old map remaining in place. If a state gained one or more seats, it could choose to elect its new allotment of members at large. If it lost any seats, it could elect all of its members at large (a much less attractive and infrequently used option). In recent decades, states have faced a very different default position, one defined by the courts.[34] Moreover, quite apart from failure to produce a plan, virtually all redistricting maps were now subject to challenge in the courts by aggrieved parties. The strategic behavior of politicians in redrawing district lines has been increasingly shaped by the prospect of judicial intervention.[35]

A number of states subsequently enacted provisions for a specific role for the courts. Some require the courts to draw up plans if the legislature and governor reach a political impasse.[36] At least one state—Colorado—calls for immediate judicial review of redistricting plans as soon as they are enacted, obviating the need for others to file suit.[37]

Rather than looking to the courts, some states remove authority and responsibility from the legislature, placing it instead in the hands of another group of actors, a panel usually referred to as an independent redistricting commission. Commissions—the most ambitious and potentially most effective reform of redistricting procedures—are invested with first and final authority in congressional redistricting by six states (Arizona, Hawaii, Idaho, Montana, New Jersey, and Washington) and in state legislative redistricting by eleven states. They are used as backup if the legislative process fails in drawing a congressional plan in one state (Indiana) and in drawing a state legislative plan in six states.[38] Other states (including Maine and Connecticut) employ commissions in an advisory capacity: their plans must be approved by the legislature before taking effect. And one state—Iowa—delegates authority for drafting congressional and state legislative redistricting plans to a nonpartisan legislative support staff agency. As discussed below, however, the Iowa legislature retains the authority to put its own mark on the ultimate plans.

Commissions presently in use for congressional and state legislative redistricting vary in size, appointment of an even or odd number of members, criteria and method used to appoint members, state redistricting standards, limits on information used in drawing plans, transparency requirements, approval of plans by majority or supermajority rule, degree of independence from the legislature and governor, provisions for judicial review, timetable for action, staff, funding, and backup provisions if the commission fails to approve a plan.[39] Not surprisingly, commissions usually produce redistricting plans that reflect their structure and rules.[40] Those with partisan majorities and simple majority rules tend to produce partisan plans. Those with evenly divided bipartisan memberships or supermajority rules or both are more likely to produce plans that protect both parties and their incumbents. Designing a commission that is neutral toward or that dampens the influence of both incumbents and parties is a challenge with which few states have successfully grappled. The experience of several states is detailed below.

Iowa

Based on its reputation for using an "independent redistricting commission" that produces strikingly competitive legislative districts, Iowa is more frequently offered as a model for redistricting reform than any other state. The underlying reality is a good deal more complicated. The Hawkeye State embraces a uniquely nonpartisan redistricting process, one in which responsibility for drawing maps is delegated to a legislative support staff office, the Legislative Services Agency (LSA), formerly the Legislative Service Bureau, but in which ultimate redistricting authority is retained by the legislature. A five-member commission is responsible for advising the agency, but only on request by the LSA. The LSA is charged with submitting up to three plans to the legislature, any of which can be approved by majority vote and signed into law by the governor. The legislature may make only technical adjustments in the first two plans, but it is free, after rejecting the first two, to make substantive changes in the third, effectively drawing its own map.[41]

The LSA must draw up its plans following four criteria (population equality, contiguity, unity of counties and cities, and compactness), without regard to political affiliation, previous election results, the addresses of incumbents, or any demographic information other than population not otherwise required by law. In this respect, the process requires redistricting to be blind to incumbency and party. But such a neutral process need not produce neutral results. In 1991 the Democratically controlled legislature approved a plan that led to major Republican gains in the subsequent election, gains that the Republicans have never relinquished. The congressional redistricting plan approved in 2001 by the Republican legislature (subject to veto by the Democratic governor) led to competitive races in four of the five districts, all of which nonetheless reelected incumbents. The legislature has never chosen to exercise its authority to draw its own maps, even when a majority believed that the neutral process had produced a partisan outcome. It appears that the "good government" norms in the state and the popularity of the nonpartisan redistricting process have constrained the self-interested behavior of incumbents and parties. It bears noting, however, that in 1981, when Republican leaders complained that two of their House incumbents were thrown together in a Democratic-leaning district, the "problem" was ameliorated in the second and ultimately successful third plan.[42]

Is Iowa a model for other states? Its historical record certainly suggests many strengths: timely completion of redistricting, no court challenges, mostly competitive seats, and no blatant incumbent or partisan gerrymandering. On the other hand, Iowa is an outlier among states. Its mix of social and geographical characteristics and close partisan balance naturally supports more competitive legislative districts. The absence of racial minorities removes all of the complicated considerations of the Voting Rights Act. Iowa's strong tradition of progressive nonpartisanship supports the unusual practice of delegating responsibility to professional staff (unusual in the United States, though not in other countries accustomed to using civil service boundary commissions) and the legislature's restraint from using its full authority to control redistricting. Finally, blind redistricting performed by nonpartisan bodies can produce undesired outcomes, even more so in states with more diverse populations and geography.

Washington

After an especially contentious post-1980 round of redistricting, the Washington legislature adopted a constitutional amendment, subsequently approved by the electorate, establishing a state redistricting commission to open its doors in 1991.[43] (A temporary commission was used in 1983 to resolve conflict over the post-1980 maps.) The amendment called for a four-member commission, divided evenly between the two parties, with a fifth nonvoting member chosen by the other commissioners to serve as chairperson. Voting members are appointed by legislative party leaders but cannot be drawn from recent, current, or prospective lobbyists or elected officials. (That restriction has not prevented the appointment of seasoned political professionals, including former legislative and party leaders. In this sense the commission is properly viewed as bipartisan, not nonpartisan.) The commission must approve its plan by supermajority vote (at least three of four votes). The proposal then goes to the legislature, which may amend within limits (but not kill) the plan by a two-thirds vote. The governor has no veto power. If the commission fails to produce a plan, the task falls to the state supreme court.

The commission operates under a number of familiar standards: equal population, contiguity, compactness, convenience, and respect for political subdivisions, communities of interest, and geographic barriers. In addition, the plan cannot favor or purposely discriminate against a party or group and should encourage electoral competition.[44]

The Washington state commission seems to be structured to avoid partisan gerrymanders and to protect the interests of incumbents. The evenly divided membership and supermajority votes required to approve or amend a plan encourage bipartisan negotiation and accommodate incumbents. Butler and Cain characterize this structure as consensual, one likely to produce bipartisan or incumbent-oriented plans.[45] Yet Washington's congressional elections were among the nation's most competitive in the decade following the post-1990 commission redistricting plan. By one measure of district partisanship, neither party was projected to win more than 52 percent of the vote in six of the state's nine congressional districts.[46] District boundaries permitted an unusually high level of responsiveness to the strong Republican tide of 1994. The delegation switched from a seven-seat Democratic advantage to a five-seat Republican margin, and seven of the nine House races were won with less than 60 percent of the vote. A less dramatic but strikingly competitive pattern continued in the subsequent three elections. In contrast, the post-2000 plan approved by the commission was followed by a pattern of House election results in the state that mirrored those in the country: every incumbent in the delegation was reelected, as were all but four House incumbents facing challengers nationwide. Yet the underlying partisan structure of the Washington congressional districts remained competitive. Four of the nine districts reelected House incumbents with less than 60 percent of the vote. More tellingly, six of the nine districts were highly competitive when measured by the 2000 presidential vote under the new district boundaries.

It is not obvious what features of the Washington redistricting process encouraged a relatively high level of responsiveness and competitiveness, in spite of the bipartisan commission membership and supermajority rules. Explicit standards encouraging electoral competition and prohibiting favorable or discriminatory treatment of a political party might be important, as might the transparent process followed by the commission, including the practice of holding extensive public hearings. It is also possible that the political and social makeup of the state—including the small percentage of racial minorities, the evenly balanced parties statewide, a populist political culture, and a tradition of no registration by party—contributed to more competitive plans than might have been expected.

New Jersey

The highly partisan state of New Jersey has used a commission to redraw its state legislative districts since 1966 and its congressional districts since 1991. The state legislative redistricting process involves the appointment of a partisan but evenly divided ten-member commission, with half of the members chosen by each of the state party chairs.[47] Current members of the legislature are eligible for appointment. If the commission fails to reach agreement by majority vote within a month, the chief justice of the state supreme court appoints an eleventh, public member, who then has one additional month to forge a majority on behalf of a plan. Based on his experience as the public, "tiebreaking" member in 1981 and 1991, Donald Stokes has recounted how this system largely succeeded in producing maps low in partisan bias and high in responsiveness to shifts in voter preferences.[48] A similar outcome was achieved in 2001 under public member Larry Bartels.[49]

The commission system in place for congressional mapmaking, adopted in 1991 by a lame duck Democratic legislature that rushed to avoid allowing redistricting authority to be exercised by the incoming Republican majority, differs from the state district process in several important respects. Each party appoints six members, who in turn elect a thirteenth, independent member by majority vote to serve as a neutral, tiebreaking chairman of the commission. The timetable and process appear to limit the public member to choosing between the two plans with the widest support, in contrast with the choice allowed Stokes, who was able to fashion an independent plan and encourage the parties to move toward it. In 1991 public member Alan Rosenthal judged the Republican plan to be fairer and cast his tiebreaking vote for it. In 2001 Rosenthal endorsed a bipartisan map proposed by the state's congressional delegation.[50] The New Jersey commission for congressional redistricting has avoided a blatant post-1980–style partisan gerrymander during both rounds that it has been in effect, which was the major objective of the new process and the highest priority identified by Rosenthal. Yet it has done little to increase competitiveness and responsiveness. In fact, incumbent protection was openly identified by both parties as a prime objective in redistricting, one that would serve the interests of New Jersey.[51] The state's congressional delegation has remained stable and roughly balanced between the parties, with only two or three of its thirteen incumbents facing any semblance of competition.

Do procedural differences alone account for the divergent outcomes of state legislative and congressional redistricting in New Jersey? There were many similarities. Both commissions were dominated by politicians and operated in a political culture that takes as a given that redistricting is an inherently political process. Neither was constrained by redistricting standards promoting competition or partisan fairness nor by requirements for public hearings. Both had tiebreaking members, and decisions were made by simple majority vote.

What was most distinct about the two types of redistricting in New Jersey was the perceived stakes. Control of the legislature was at risk in the state redistricting process, not so for congressional redistricting. Party control of a state delegation to the U.S. House carries few benefits, and minor shifts in the partisan composition of the New Jersey House delegation are unlikely to affect which party is in the majority in Washington. That encourages bipartisan collaboration in maintaining the status quo. The potential consequences of state and congressional redistricting and therefore the incentives for mapmakers are very different. Those who draw state legislative districts are likely to produce competing partisan plans and an opportunity for the public, tiebreaking member to make a real difference.

Arizona

The latest and most ambitious exercise in redistricting reform was authorized by popular initiative in Arizona in 2000. Proposition 106 amended the Arizona constitution to vest authority for redrawing the state's congressional and legislative districts in a five-member commission.[52] Four members (two from each party) are appointed by legislative leaders from a pool of nominees approved by the Commission on Appellate Court Appointments. These nominees must be registered Arizona voters who have not recently been elected or appointed to public or party office. The four appointees then choose a fifth member from a comparable pool of nominees not affiliated with either of the two major parties. Commission maps approved by majority vote are not subject to review by the legislature or veto by the governor.

The Arizona constitution is explicit about the standards and procedures the commission must follow in creating redistricting plans:

The independent redistricting commission shall establish congressional and legislative districts. The commencement of the mapping process for both the congressional and legislative districts shall be the creation of districts of equal population in a grid-like pattern across the state. Adjustments to the grid shall then be made as necessary to accommodate the goals as set forth below:

A. Districts shall comply with the United States Constitution and the United States voting rights act;

B. Congressional districts shall have equal population to the extent practicable, and state legislative districts shall have equal population to the extent practicable;

C. Districts shall be geographically compact and contiguous to the extent practicable;

D. District boundaries shall respect communities of interest to the extent practicable;

E. To the extent practicable, district lines shall use visible geographic features, city, town and county boundaries, and undivided census tracts;

F. To the extent practicable, competitive districts should be favored where to do so would create no significant detriment to the other goals.

(15) Party registration and voting history data shall be excluded from the initial phase of the mapping process but may be used to test maps for compliance with the above goals. The places of residence of incumbents or candidates shall not be identified or considered.[53]

The commission's initial experience in drawing congressional and legislative maps under these procedures and standards reveals the difficulty of achieving all of the desired objectives. Arizona has a rapidly growing population, which, combined with the even more explosive growth of Hispanics in the state, is producing an increasingly competitive statewide political environment. Creating additional competitive districts (which in this case means more opportunities for Democrats to compete) is constrained by the need to adhere to VRA requirements and to respect communities of interest. Given the geographical distribution of Democratic and Republican voters, drawing compact districts in a gridlike pattern can frustrate the achievement of other important redistricting objectives.

Election returns in 2002 suggest a modest gain in competitiveness, one that is more apparent when the presidential vote is used to control the advantages of House incumbency. Democrats marginally improved their standing in a delegation dominated by Republicans. A second majority-minority district produced the expected outcome—the election of a Hispanic Democrat. But the result fell well short of what many commission proponents and Democrats had hoped, leading to court challenges, which at the congressional level were decided in favor of the commission.

Steven Lynn, chair of the Arizona redistricting commission, argues that the new process achieved its most important objective, which was the basis on which it had been sold to the public in the initiative election: the people drew the lines, not the politicians in the legislature.[54] The commission was genuinely independent and conducted its work in a highly transparent fashion.

Lessons from Commissions

Lessons from the preceding brief case studies and from other analyses of the structure and outcome of redistricting commissions suggest both the limits and possibilities of this reform genre. A commission can be used as efficiently as the normal legislative process to achieve partisan or incumbent-protecting gerrymanders. A commission controlled through appointment by the majority party in the legislature and operating under simple majority rule will find it very difficult to exercise independent judgment. Partisan plans are their likely product. On the other hand, a commission whose membership is evenly divided between the parties or whose maps must be adopted by a supermajority vote or both is naturally drawn toward bipartisan compromise, which usually works to the advantage of incumbents and to the detriment of competition. Independent, tiebreaking members under majority rule dampen partisan gerrymandering, but their impact on competition is conditioned by whether the other, partisan commissioners have incentives to collaborate.

As seen in the experiences recounted above, the relationship between commission structure and outcome is not inviolate. Other aspects of state political geography and culture and the standards and rules under which commissions operate can make a significant difference. Commissions instructed to produce plans that promote competition operate differently from those that are given no such instructions. States requiring public hearings and a more transparent mapmaking process will find their commissions avoiding some of the more obvious redistricting traps. Specific provisions that balance partisan representation and insulation from undue political influence can be critical in shaping the work of a commission. The political circumstances under which a redistricting commission is authorized—by popular initiative, a court mandate, a lame duck state legislative majority, or a bipartisan agreement—can matter as well.

While it is probably a mistake to search for a model redistricting commission that is appropriate for use in all states, there are a number of critical design issues that ought to be addressed by commission advocates. A number of individuals and organizations have crafted recommendations for the structure and operation of commissions. Michael McDonald draws on the Arizona experience and his broader scholarly work to offer redistricting commission guidelines that he believes are most likely to increase competitiveness.[55] Common Cause recently issued its own set of redistricting guidelines.[56] And in connection with Governor Arnold Schwarzenegger's proposal to give redistricting authority in California to a panel of retired judges, the Center for Governmental Studies and Demos released a comprehensive guide to redistricting reform and an evaluation of several legislative bills and initiatives to create an independent redistricting commission in the state.[57] While these three sets of recommendations overlap in many respects, there are also substantial areas of disagreement.

Commission Size, Composition, and Voting Rules

One important point of consensus among these sets of guidelines is that to avoid stalemate, commissions should have an odd number of members.[58] Commission size is another matter, depending mainly on the importance attached to representing racial and ethnic stakeholders. How best to avoid undue political influence while ensuring partisan representation and fairness? Allow for an equal number of partisan appointees from each major party from a pool that removes recent and current elected and party officials and prohibits commission members from seeking office in the newly created legislative districts. These appointees should then select a tiebreaking member from a pool of individuals not associated with either political party.

Some advocates, partial to an Iowa-style nonpartisan redistricting agency, prefer to remove rather than equalize partisan interests. In their view, an entirely "blind" process is most likely to diminish party and incumbent advantages. Experience suggests otherwise. Neutral players following apolitical rules do not necessarily produce neutral outcomes.

Should commissions decide on plans by majority or by supermajority rule? The risk of the latter is that it favors bipartisan, anticompetitive plans. While that risk might be mitigated by other rules and standards governing the commission, majority rule under the appointment procedure outlined above offers a more promising alternative for balancing partisan fairness and competitiveness.

Redistricting Standards

Commissions will perforce operate under the constitutional and federal statutory requirements of equal population and minority representation. Less obvious is the priority that ought to be attached to traditional state redistricting standards—contiguity, compactness, governmental boundaries, and communities of interest—relative to that attached to the more explicitly political standards of partisan fairness and competitiveness. Given the high degree of geographical segregation of like-minded citizens, compactness and communities of interest can work directly against competitiveness. Asking a commission to adhere to traditional redistricting standards, then, may undermine a primary goal of many reform efforts.

Will removing opportunities for partisan and incumbent mischief by creating an independent redistricting commission be sufficient to achieve the desired objectives of partisan fairness and competitiveness, or should an explicit and high priority be given to those objectives? Experience suggests that both partisan fairness and competitiveness should be included as essential standards for redistricting commissions. Moreover, a robust definition of partisan fairness—one that includes both a lack of bias (neither party should have an advantage in controlling a majority of seats if there is a dead heat in the popular vote) and responsiveness (a shift in the popular vote off a dead heat should lead the party favored by that shift to build up a majority of seats)—provides an indirect means of increasing competitiveness.[59] By itself, competitiveness is a difficult standard to meet in redistricting: How should it be measured? Should it be based solely on a generic measure of party strength or take account of the incumbent as well? What percentage of a state's districts should be competitive?

Redistricting Processes

Commission architects should ensure a fully transparent process, with adequate time for public input and public review of draft commission plans; funding sufficient to allow independent work free of political interference; provision for immediate review by the state supreme court in order to avoid having plans get stuck in a legal quagmire; and, absent a court order, prohibition of more than a single round of redistricting each decade. A final consideration is the information made available to the commission in drawing its maps. Denying the commission knowledge of where incumbents reside reduces opportunities for anticompetitive mischief; it also directly challenges the view, supported by court decisions, that incumbency is a state resource that can be protected legitimately in the redistricting process. The trade-off between these competing values may well argue for an incumbent-blind process, although it is a very close call. Access to partisan voting and registration data, on the other hand, is essential to formulating various plans and evaluating their success in achieving partisan fairness and increased competitiveness.

Conclusion

Gerrymandering is but one of the forces responsible for the ills associated with contemporary congressional elections, from the decline of competitive seats to the growing ideological polarization of the parties. Evidence presented in this volume and elsewhere confirms the conclusion that many factors—including the geographical movement of voters, the regional realignment of the parties, and the advantages of incumbency—contribute to those maladies.⁶⁰ Redistricting reform, therefore, is no panacea for the problems of polarization and lack of competitiveness in national politics.

On the other hand, it is not an unreasonable place to start. It would be foolish to deny the reality that changes in incentives and resources have combined to produce ever more egregious manifestations of self-dealing in the redistricting process by parties and elected officials. The redistricting world of weak parties and decentralized politics described by Butler and Cain has been replaced by one with strong and aggressive national parties choreographing developments in the states.⁶¹ The self-regulating zero-sum game between partisan and incumbent-protecting gerrymandering that limited the damage from self-interested behavior has become a largely positive-sum game. James Madison, who had to overcome a district gerrymandered against him in his first run for Congress, would nonetheless be appalled to see how those in power are able to perpetuate their standing by manipulating the electoral rules of the game—and to see how blatantly they ignore this conflict of interest.

As Donald Stokes has argued persuasively, there are methods of redistricting that lie somewhere between an entirely neutral, apolitical process, one "notably short on practical wisdom," and "the American practice of leaving the drawing of boundaries to the ordinary political process, with results that are notably short on public interest."⁶² This chapter has suggested some of the levers for change in the redistricting process—Congress, the courts, state legislatures, and the popular initiative—and alternative redistricting standards and processes that might encourage a constructive mix of practical wisdom and public interest.

Given the natural tendency of politicians to avoid relinquishing any element of control over their political future, constructive reform is most likely to originate from the popular initiative process, currently in place in twenty-four states. Efforts to establish independent redistricting commissions, modeled at least in part on the successful 2000 Arizona initiative, are under way in at least a half-dozen states. Success in several of these states could spill over into others, eventually building pressure on Congress, state legislatures, and the courts to respond to growing demand to dilute incumbent politicians' influence in drawing district lines.

The years leading up to the 2010 census and reapportionment should be a time of institutional innovation in legislative mapmaking, one that permits state experimentation with a wide range of alternative processes and standards. That would facilitate a more informed analysis of the links among competition, partisanship, and redistricting and set the stage for broader changes in the electoral system that might well enhance the legitimacy of American democracy.

Notes

1. David Butler and Bruce Cain, *Congressional Redistricting: Comparative and Theoretical Perspectives* (New York: Macmillan, 1992), chapter 6.

2. As Dennis Thompson points out, however, James Madison would not approve. He distinguished ordinary legislation from electoral regulation. On the latter, the normal process of representation served to preserve the privileges of incumbents and perpetuate the practices of the institution. Dennis F. Thompson, "Election Time: Normative Implications of Temporal Properties of the Electoral Process in the United States," *American Political Science Review* 98 (February 2004): 51–64.

3. E. J. Dionne Jr., *Why Americans Hate Politics* (New York: Simon and Schuster, 1992): 357.

4. Thomas E. Mann, "Linking Knowledge and Action: Political Science and Campaign Finance Reform," *Perspectives on Politics* 1 (March 2003): 69–83.

5. See Anthony Corrado, Thomas E. Mann, and Trevor Potter, eds., *Inside the Campaign Finance Battle: Court Testimony on the New Reforms* (Brookings, 2003); and Daniel H. Lowenstein and Richard L. Hasen, eds., "Symposium: *McConnell v. Federal Election Commission*," *Election Law Journal* 3, no. 2 (2004): 115–369.

6. Anthony Corrado, "Party Finance in the Wake of BCRA: An Overview," in *The Election after Reform: Money, Politics, and the Bipartisan Campaign Reform Act*, edited by Michael J. Malbin (Lanham, Md.: Rowman and Littlefield, 2005).

7. Thompson, "Election Time," p. 54.

8. Jamie L. Carson and Michael H. Crespin, "The Effect of State Redistricting Methods on Electoral Competition in United States House of Representatives Races," *State Politics and Policy Quarterly* 4 (Winter 2004): 455–69; Sam Hirsch, "The United States House of Unrepresentatives: What Went Wrong in the Latest Round of Congressional Redistricting," *Election Law Journal* 2, no. 2 (2003): 179–216.

9. I have found two sources especially helpful in conceptualizing the objectives and alternatives in redistricting reform: Butler and Cain, *Congressional Redistricting*, chapter 7; and Michael P. McDonald, "Enhancing Competitiveness in Redistricting" (http://elections.gmu.edu/enhancing.htm [April 12, 2004]).

10. Butler and Cain, *Congressional Redistricting*, p. 125; Center for Voting and Democracy (www.fairvote.org/redistricting/ [April 12, 2004]).

11. Andrew Hacker, *Congressional Districting: The Issue of Equal Representation* (Brookings, 1963), pp. 6–7; Laurence F. Schmeckebier, *Congressional Apportionment* (Westport, Conn.: Greenwood Press, 1941), p. 132.

12. 5 Stat. 491 (1842).

13. 46 Stat. 13 (1929).

14. 81 Stat. 581 (1967), codified at 2 U.S.C 2c.

15. Gary W. Cox, *Making Votes Count: Strategic Coordination in the World's Electoral Systems* (Cambridge University Press, 1997); Samuel Issacharoff, Pamela S. Karlan, and Richard H. Pildes, *The Law of Democracy: Legal Structure of the Political Process*, 2d ed. (Westbury, N.Y.: Foundation Press, 2001), pp. 1160–67; Douglas W. Rae, *The Political Consequences of Electoral Laws* (Yale University Press, 1967).

16. Center for Voting and Democracy (www.fairvote.org/irv/ [April 7, 2005]).

17. 5 Stat. 491 (1842); 9 Stat. 433 (1850); 12 Stat. 572 (1862); 17 Stat. 28 (1872); 22 Stat. 5 (1882); 26 Stat. 735 (1891); 31 Stat. 733 (1901); 37 Stat. 13 (1911).

18. Joel Francis Paschal, "The House of Representatives: 'Grand Depository of the Democratic Principle'?" *Law and Contemporary Problems* 17 (1952): 276–89; Schmeckebier, *Congressional Apportionment,* pp. 135–38.

19. Thomas M. Durbin and L. Paige Whitaker, "Congressional and State Reapportionment and Redistricting: A Legal Analysis," *CRS Report for Congress,* September 4, 1996, pp. 5–6.

20. Richard L. Hasen, *The Supreme Court and Election Law: Judging Equality from Baker v. Carr to Bush v. Gore* (New York University Press, 2003); Hirsch, "The United States House of Unrepresentatives."

21. Alan Ehrenhalt, "Frankfurter's Curse," *Governing* 17, no. 4 (January 2004): 4–7.

22. *Davis* v. *Bandemer,* 478 U.S. 109, 133 (1986).

23. *Vieth* v. *Jubelirer,* 541 U.S. 267 (2004).

24. Most recently, the U.S. Supreme Court vacated a district court decision and remanded the Texas case *Session* v. *Perry* to the lower court "for further consideration in light of *Vieth* v. *Jubelirer*" (Civil Action no. 2:03-CV-354).

25. Richard L. Hasen, "Looking for Standards (in All the Wrong Places): Partisan Gerrymandering Claims after *Vieth,*" *Election Law Journal* 3, no. 4 (2004): 626–42. A more optimistic view of a future role for the courts is contained in Mitchell N. Berman, "Managing Gerrymandering," *Texas Law Review* 83 (February 2005): 781–854.

26. Samuel Isaacharoff, "Gerrymandering and Political Cartels," *Harvard Law Review* 116 (December 2002): 593–648.

27. Hasen, *The Supreme Court and Election Law;* Nathaniel Persily, "In Defense of Foxes Guarding Henhouses: The Case for Judicial Acquiescence to Incumbent-Protecting Gerrymanders," *Harvard Law Review* 116 (December 2002): 649–83.

28. *Burns* v. *Richardson,* 384 U.S. 73, 89 (1966); *White* v. *Weiser,* 412 U.S. 783, 791, 797 (1973).

29. For another perspective, see Hirsch, "The United States House of Unrepresentatives."

30. McDonald, "Enhancing Competitiveness in Redistricting."

31. Butler and Cain, *Congressional Redistricting;* McDonald, "Enhancing Competitiveness in Redistricting."

32. Michael P. McDonald, "A Comparative Analysis of Redistricting Institutions in the United States, 2001–02," *State Politics and Policy Quarterly* 4 (Winter 2004): 371–95.

33. Bruce E. Cain, *The Reapportionment Puzzle* (University of California Press, 1984).

34. Gary W. Cox and Jonathan N. Katz, *Elbridge Gerry's Salamander: The Electoral Consequences of the Reapportionment Revolution* (Cambridge University Press, 2002).

35. Ibid.

36. Butler and Cain, *Congressional Redistricting,* pp. 110–15, 147–48.

37. Jeffrey C. Kubin, "The Case for Redistricting Commissions," *Texas Law Review* 75 (March 1997): 850.

38. McDonald, "Comparative Analysis of Redistricting Institutions."

39. Butler and Cain, *Congressional Redistricting;* Bruce E. Cain and David A. Hopkins, "Mapmaking at the Grassroots: The Legal and Political Issues of Local Redistricting," *Election Law Journal* 1, no. 4 (2002); Hirsch, "The United States House of Unrepresentatives; Sam Hirsch, "Unpacking *Page* v. *Bartels*: A Fresh Redistricting Paradigm Emerges in New Jersey," *Election Law Journal* 1, no. 1 (2002); Kubin, "The Case for Redistricting Commissions"; McDonald, "Enhancing Competitiveness in Redistricting"; Persily, "In Defense of Foxes Guarding Henhouses."

40. McDonald, "Comparative Analysis of Redistricting Institutions."

41. Iowa State Constitution, art. III, sec. 37.

42. Alan Ehrenhalt, "Reapportionment and Redistricting," in *The American Elections of 1982,* edited by Thomas E. Mann and Norman J. Ornstein (Washington: American Enterprise Institute, 1983), p. 55.

43. Washington Secretary of State (www.secstate.wa.gov/oralhistory/redistricting/1980s/ [April 12, 2004]).

44. Washington State Constitution, sec. 43, part 5.

45. Butler and Cain, *Congressional Redistricting*, p. 151.

46. Center for Voting and Democracy, "Washington's Redistricting Information" (www.fairvote. org/redistricting/reports/remanual/frames.htm [April 12, 2004]).

47. Donald E. Stokes, "Is There a Better Way to Redistrict?" in *Race and Redistricting in the 1990s*, edited by Bernard Grofman (New York: Agathon Press, 1998), pp. 345–66.

48. Stokes, "Is There a Better Way to Redistrict?"

49. Hirsch, "Unpacking *Page* v. *Bartels*," pp. 7–23.

50. McDonald, "Comparative Analysis of Redistricting Institutions."

51. Donald Scarinci and Nomi Lowy, "Congressional Redistricting in New Jersey," *Seton Hall Law Review* 32 (2003): 821–35.

52. Arizona Secretary of State, 2000 Voter's Pamphlet (www.sosaz.com/election/2000/Info/ pubpamphlet/english/prop106.pdf [April 12, 2004]).

53. Arizona State Constitution, art. IV.

54. See the transcript for "Panel 4: Alternatives to Traditional Redistricting Processes" of the Brookings Institution/Institute of Governmental Studies conference "Competition, Partisanship, and Congressional Redistricting," Brookings Institution, Washington, April 16, 2004 (www.brook.edu/gs/crc_Panel_4.pdf [April 7, 2005]).

55. McDonald, "Enhancing Competitiveness in Redistricting."

56. "Common Cause Redistricting Guidelines," February 2005 (www.commoncause.org/site/ pp.asp?c=dkLNK1MQIwG&b=366007 [April 7, 2005]).

57. Ari Weisbard and Jeannie Wilkinson, "Drawing Lines: A Public Interest Guide to Real Redistricting Reform," Center for Governmental Studies and Demos, February 2005 (www.cgs. org/publications/docs/DrawingLinesAPublicInterestGuidetoRedistrictingReform.pdf [April 7, 2005]); "Addendum to Drawing Lines: A Public Interest Guide to Real Redistricting Reform," Center for Governmental Studies and Demos, March 2005 (www.cgs.org/publications/docs/ DrawingLinesAddendumMarch2005Final.pdf [April 7, 2005]).

58. Note that Washington, with four voting commissioners, has nonetheless managed to produce plans in the last two rounds of redistricting.

59. Stokes, "Is There a Better Way to Redistrict?"

60. See, for example, a fascinating article demonstrating how a striking partisan divide has developed at the county level, which is not subject to the mapmaking manipulation of politicians: Bill Bishop, "The Schism in U.S. Politics Begins at Home," *Austin American-Statesman*, April 4, 2004. See also Alan I. Abramowitz, Brad Alexander, and Matthew Gunning, "Incumbency, Redistricting, and the Decline of Competition in U.S. House Elections," presented at the Annual Meeting of the Southern Political Science Association, New Orleans, Louisiana, January 6–8, 2005.

61. Butler and Cain, *Congressional Redistricting*.

62. Stokes, "Is There a Better Way to Redistrict?" p. 345.

Contributors

Micah Altman, *Harvard University*

Bruce E. Cain, *University of California, Berkeley*

Karin Mac Donald, *University of California, Berkeley*

Cherie D. Maestas, *Florida State University*

L. Sandy Maisel, *Colby College*

Thomas E. Mann, *Brookings Institution*

Michael McDonald, *George Mason University*

Nathaniel Persily, *University of Pennsylvania*

Walter J. Stone, *University of California, Davis*

Index